Impermanent
Immortality

2012 • IMPERMANENT IMMORTALITY

2011 • AT THE MERCY OF THE ELEMENTS

2010 • THAT RASCAL MIND

2008 • PASSACAGLIA ON PASSING

2007 • OFF THE BEATEN TRACK

2006 • SCATTERED CLOUDS

2005 • ROASTED CHESTNUTS

2003 • HOT FLASHES

2002 • LIGHT FINGERS

1999 • INDIA JOURNAL

# Impermanent Immortality

CHERYL WILFONG

HEART PATH PRESS
2012

Cheryl Wilfong
Heart Path Press, L3C
314 Partridge Road
Putney VT 05346

www.meditativegardener.com

©2012 Cheryl Wilfong
All rights reserved. No part of this book may be
reproduced in any form or by any means, electronic
or mechanical, including photocopying, recording,
or by any information storage and retrieval system,
without permission in writing from the publisher.

ISBN: 978-0-9825664-4-2

*Follow* The Meditative Gardener *on Facebook*

*My Dear Friend,*

Welcome to this year's collection of reflections on life. My daily, mundane life offers lots of opportunities for reflections, as I'm sure yours does too.

We'd like to leave our mark on life, yet, if we turn our back for just a minute, we find our footprints in the sand of life washing away behind us. When even the Roy Rogers Museum had to close, due to low attendance, we can see that immortality is indeed impermanent.

Because we each experience our own private world, I offer this perennial reminder:

> **WARNING!**
> You may think you know some of the people in these stories.
> But if you ask the people with those names, you'll hear a completely different story.

Thanks to Mike Fleming for editing. His good ideas when I felt stuck, his attention to detail, and his insistence on my trademark endings means that you, the reader, aren't left stranded. Deep appreciation to this book's designer, Carolyn Kasper.

Thanks to you, dear friend, for reading,

cheryl.wilfong@gmail.com

# Contents

My Immortality Project     1

## Bill and Cheryl
## 5

| | |
|---|---:|
| October Snow | 7 |
| The Kitchen Sponge | 16 |
| Bill's Computers | 18 |
| Honey Woman | 20 |
| Do-It-Yourself | 22 |
| Cooperation | 27 |
| Report Card on Life | 30 |
| Cold and Hot Sleeping | 32 |

## Best of the Blog 2012
## The Ten Supremes
## 35

## At Home
## 75

| | |
|---|---:|
| My iPhone Is My Bible | 77 |
| Jewel Tones | 80 |
| Live It Loud | 82 |
| Daylilies | 84 |
| Partridge Road on Spring Equinox: Nine Houses, Three Seasons, One Road | 86 |
| Run-Ins | 88 |
| My Medicare Card | 90 |
| Buying a Second Home | 92 |
| The To-Do List | 94 |
| Waking Up | 97 |
| Pen-Challenged | 100 |
| Living (and Sleeping) with Restless Legs | 102 |
| Lost | 106 |
| Love Changes | 109 |
| Free as a Bird | 111 |
| Great Blue Heron | 113 |
| Compost Pile | 115 |

## Best of the Blog 2012
## Impermanence
## 117

## Cheryl's Memories
### 135

| | |
|---|---|
| Mackinac | 137 |
| Things I Believed Were True When I Was a Child | 140 |
| Recipes from Ten-Year-Old Cheryl | 142 |
| Wild Strawberries | 147 |
| Nonnie's Fingers | 148 |
| May 1, 2011 | 150 |
| A Narrow Life | 153 |
| My 45th High School Reunion | 156 |

## Endings
### 161

| | |
|---|---|
| Don't Panic | 163 |
| Body Trill | 165 |
| What Do the Dying See? | 167 |
| Wind on the Lake | 169 |
| Plop! | 172 |
| I, Too | 175 |
| The Six-Year Hospice Patient | 178 |

# My Immortality Project

I'm working on this year's vanity book, culling through my writing of the past twelve months. First, there's the rereading what I've written and deciding thumbs up or thumbs down, then there's the typing, and then there's three weeks of editing. Really, I should offer a workshop for writers who want to have a finished product.

Meanwhile, I'm wondering: *Do I even want to finish this product?* After all, a vanity book is so vain—it's all about me. My editor tells me I need to call it something else, that it's more than a vanity book.

What could I call it? ? A chapbook? But "chapbook" usually refers to poetry. I could call it a book of essays. Or what do you call a blog in hard-copy? A log? A journal?

I never really know how it's going to turn out, though some sections recur every year: Bill, Travel, Nature, Death, and my own op-ed pieces.

Otto Rank, an early-twentieth-century psychoanalyst, would call it my Immortality Project. Each one of us has an Immortality Project as a way of staving off the reality of death. Children are the most prevalent Immortality Project, and artistic expression is also quite common.

My friend, Trudy, paints one painting a day. She's 87, and wonders what will happen to her piles and piles of watercolors, temperas, and oil paintings when she dies or has to move out of her house.

In early December of every year, she invites friends over to her house to look through her portfolio for the year. She sells most of her paintings for $10 or $15. I already have a dozen; I call it my Trudy Gallery.

Trudy has four daughters and seven grandchildren. Maybe they'll divide up her paintings, or maybe they'll throw them in the dumpster. Vincent van Gogh's mother threw away several of his paintings. Sometimes immortality doesn't last very long, even after you've spent your whole life working on it and organizing it. Immortality is impermanent.

I put this book together partly because I'd like to know about my own parents, grandparents, and greats. Who were those people anyway? What kind of person was the Grandmom who died when I was sixteen? And after spending my entire lifetime with my parents, they died, and I realized I didn't really know them as people. Who were they, anyway? What were they like when they were young? Which of life's lessons would they pass on to me if they could?

On the egotistical assumption that at least one of my nieces or nephews will feel this same empty longing, I publish this book of reflections and send it off like a message in a bottle floating in oceans of stuff. "Save me. Save my name, my personality, my sense of personhood, my sense of self. I'm marooned on this desert island called Life, and I'm reaching out to you, O Unknown Reader, hoping you will say, "Now, there's a person I would like to have known." And even if you say, "Brother, what an idiot," I'll be dead and won't know the difference.

Readers of my little books like to read them because they know me and they come to know me much more intimately through the reading of my thoughts and perceptions of everyday life. Because I love history—I even wrote a history book[1]—I hope a future reader will find the history represented by these period pieces inherently interesting. But history is just the Immortality Project of our culture, our society, leading us to believe in certain myths.

So I leave it to you, my present-day readers, to tell me what the heck I'm doing, spending two months of every year focused on an Immortality Project that will, upon my death (or even before), just be thrown into the dumpster.

---

[1] *Following the Nez Perce Trail: A Guide to the Nee-Me-Poo National Historic Trail with Eyewitness Accounts*, 2nd ed. (Corvallis, OR: Oregon State University Press, 2006).

Bill and Cheryl

# October Snow

My 2005 Prius without snow tires is terrible in the snow. The anti-skid device kicks in when the tires slip, and actually puts the brake on the slipping wheel. This means that even though I'm pushing the gas pedal to the floor, the car chugs up a hill, for instance, like a cog railroad. Go a few inches, slip, brake; go a few inches, slip, brake. The car is driving itself. I just happen to be sitting behind the steering wheel thinking I have my usual control over this motor vehicle. Not!

I love my Prius 360 days a year, but a couple of days every year I'm ready to kick it in the tires and leave it stranded in a snowdrift by the side of the road.

On Saturday, October 28, 2011, we drove to Boston to see the grandchildren play soccer. Max's game was at nine o'clock, which meant that we left home at six. I bundled Bill into the reclined passenger seat with his pillow and a fleece blanket. Chloe's game wasn't until 3:30, so the plan was that I would help Chloe sew the Halloween costumes—Mickey and Minnie Mouse.

I had given her a sewing machine the previous Christmas, when she was ten. The little Chinese import had its idiosyncrasies, but the other two grandmothers, who each spend one afternoon a week with the children, knew nothing about sewing machines. And Jeni, Bill's daughter (Chloe's mother), keeps her sewing kit of one needle and a spool of black thread in a plastic baggie. I hadn't seen Chloe together with her sewing machine in more than ten months, so I was chomping at the bit to get that girl back on the machine.

I had called three fabric stores asking for Minnie Mouse red-with-white-polka-dots fabric. And I had driven to the only one that said, "Yes, we have it," which happened to be in Greenfield, Massachusetts, where I was supplied with Minnie Mouse's skirt material, a matching grosgrain ribbon for her hair, and a lovely, soft, red chamois microfleece for Mickey Mouse's shorts. I added elastic and red thread to my pile of notions, and I was ready.

Jeni e-mailed that if we didn't want to come because of the weather, she'd understand.

Are you kidding? We hadn't seen those kids in ten weeks, not since we had dinner with them in Maine in August. Now, in late October, Max had just had his eighth birthday. I had his birthday present wrapped and ready to go. We weren't going to pass up a seven-hour visit just because of a little snow in the forecast.

Why, it had snowed just the week before, immediately melting off the roads and giving a nice white glaze to the landscape. Accuweather said it wouldn't get down to freezing until 8:00 p.m., so if we left Boston at four, we'd be home a little after six, safe and sound.

Max's soccer game of eight-year-olds in a little park was chilly and breezy, but we had our beach chairs and blankets to wrap up in as we watched the three red-shirted boys on each team run back and forth on the grass in a little park.

After an hour, we drove to Jeni's family condo, where Chloe and I set up her sewing machine on the dining room table. She remembered how to thread it. I set my chair off to the side, so she was in the pilot's seat. She whizzed right through Minnie's skirt; it only needed one seam. Then she got out the iron and ironing board, and she ironed and then sewed the casing for the elastic waistband. I measured Max's waist with the elastic—the plan was for both of them to cross-dress—and Chloe pulled the elastic through the waistband. Voila! Minnie (a.k.a. Max) was costumed with a white shirt, black tights, and oversized mouse shoes and white gloves from the Dollar Store.

Now for Mickey's attire. Jeni had bought a pair of men's red running shorts, but Chloe, who almost never says "No," didn't say "Yes." The gray piping down the sides just wasn't right. I turned them wrong side out. Voila! Oversized red shorts. Chloe stuck a little pillow in her tummy in order to look more mousy, but again, she didn't say "Yes."

While I waited for the verdict, I sewed up a hole in Jeni's favorite gloves.

"Let's make shorts," Chloe said. So we took a pattern that she had chosen for her birthday present three months earlier, and we laid out the brown tissue paper pieces on the red chamois microfleece.

Pockets? Or not? She decided not. My intention was to cut the side seam an extra inch wide for the oversized look, but Chloe had the scissors, and I forgot, and soon the fabric was cut for a size-12 girl.

We took a break for lunch, and then Chloe went back to the sewing machine. Why, this thing was working perfectly. What happened to those frustrating idiosyncrasies that Jeni had repeatedly called me about last January?

I did see that the wind was really blowing, but my attention was on the seams of the shorts. And then the waistband and the elastic. Chloe tried on the red shorts over black tights, and, oh my! Those shorts were cute!

Chloe said she wanted those two white dot decorations on the front of Mickey's shorts. Oh, yeah. The buttons. "Buttons?" Chloe asked me. And I saw the generation gap. The white "dots" were artifacts from Mickey's suspenders, but he hadn't worn suspenders for decades.

So I cut some stray shirt-weight cardboard into big circles, found some white fabric in Chloe's quite sizable sewing paraphernalia box, and started making the buttons. Chloe was weary by this time, and she needed to leave at 2:30 for her 3:30 soccer game. She just had time to topstitch the fabric onto the cardboard. She tried on her Mickey shorts and decided where she wanted the buttons placed. While she changed into soccer gear, I sewed the dots on the shorts. Whew! Done!

And now we were going to a soccer game in the windy rain at 43 degrees? Jeni left with Chloe, and I lay down on the sofa to rest. Bill and I left at three o'clock and arrived at the soaking soccer game at 3:30. We stayed ten minutes. Jeni agreed: it was time for us to head home.

As we approached Route 9 five minutes later, a snow squall swirled around us. *Wait a minute. It wasn't supposed to snow in Boston.* And by the time we were on Route 128, ten minutes later, Bill, who was driving my Prius, said, "Look at that! Sleet!"

I looked at the splats on the windshield. By the time we got to Route 2, fifteen minutes later, the precipitation was definitely more on the snowy side and less rainy. Driving out of Boston on Saturday in the late afternoon meant steady but not crowded traffic.

Twenty minutes later, past the town of Harvard, the passing lane became slushy. We couldn't go any faster than the 42-mph car in front of us because the slush was a bit slippery. Pickups and SUVs passed us, kicking up spray after spray of slushy wet.

"Do you think all this snow is because of Mount Wachusett?" I asked hopefully at Fitchburg. *If we could just lose some elevation, maybe the snow would turn to rain.*

"No," said Bill.

"I can hardly wait to get off Route 2," Bill said at Leominster.

"Just a few more exits to 140," I said.

Finally, exit 24 hove into view. "This is it!" I said. What that also meant was: *This is the halfway point. This is where we usually change drivers.*

Bill turn-signaled down the exit ramp, which was much snowier than the trafficked Route 2. Route 140 was just two ruts in the snow.

"Just up here," I said to Bill. "You can pull over." But the street on the right side had not been plowed. "No! Don't pull over! If the Prius gets into that much snow, we'll be stuck, and we won't be able to get ourselves out."

Bill drove on.

Now we were definitely on the shoulder of Mount Wachusett. I knew from a detour at midnight last December 17, the night I had given Chloe and Max their sewing machine, that Winchendon was surprisingly high in elevation. It had snow when neighboring towns did not.

*Why, oh why did we get off of Route 2?* Out of the frying pan and into the fire. Out of the slush and into a blizzard.

By now, I was consulting the map on my iPhone every two minutes, watching the blue ball that was our blue Prius millimetering along the highway.

"There's a motel in Winchendon," I said. "Let's stay there. Just a few more miles."

But as we approached the Countryside Motel on the south side of Winchendon, the office looked dark, and the uphill parking lot had not been plowed.

"Drive on," I said to Bill. "We'll get stuck if we try that parking lot."

Winchendon was swirling with snowflakes in streetlamp yellowish haze. A dozen cars were pulled over at Mr. Mike's Mini Mart.

Ordinarily, Winchendon means *one more hour to home*, but we'd already spent our usual two-and-a-half hours just getting this far.

We drove on. Where else could we go?

Bill began to squirm in the driver's seat. I recognized the symptoms of old man's urgency. Since his early seventies, he hasn't been able to drive to Boston without stopping at least once, and usually twice, to go to the bathroom. The urgency comes over him suddenly. In between highway exits, his bladder is about to burst. The squirming and fidgeting is just the precursor. "I've got to pee," Bill said.

"Well, you can't pull over," I said. More squirming. More fidgeting. "Here Bill," I said, "Use this Styrofoam cup."

He straightened up slightly, both hands still on the wheel in the dusky twilight.

"You'll have to unzip me," he said.

I fumbled with his zipper.

"Pull my penis out," he directed.

I reached in, took his everyday small penis in my fingers and aimed it into the cup, trying to bend it in the right direction.

"Ow. That's painful," he said. I released the nervousness from my fingers and peered closely into his lap as I heard liquid in the cup. *How much pee did he have? Would he fill the cup?*

As I squinted, I could finally see the pee-line rising, and he stopped. He sighed. I sighed. I took the cup, lowered my window, and threw the liquid out into the night, and pitched the empty cup into the back seat.

I returned to my iPhone map. The blue ball was approaching Fitzwilliam, New Hampshire. I googled "Fitzwilliam Inn." I couldn't read the small print. I reached into the back seat, groping around all the blankets, food, extra clothes, and pillows, hoping my fingers would land on my pocketbook. I didn't want to turn on the overhead light and disturb Bill's vision, which is already clouded by the beginnings of a cataract.

My pocketbook. My reading glasses. Now, what does that website say?

I pushed the numbers for the Fitzwilliam Inn and their voice mail answered. "We are open for dinner from Wednesday through Saturday."

"Turn at the blinking light, I said. "We'll go to the Fitzwilliam Inn. You've wanted to stay there, and now is our opportunity. Let's be masters of our own fate, rather than letting fate be the master of us."

Route 119 into the village had been recently plowed,

so the Prius had no problem going up the little incline. We pulled into the unplowed parking lot and simply parked on the side, just a few feet from the road.

"Maybe by the time we have dinner, the roads will be plowed," Bill said. He was thinking of his Sunday morning job, playing the organ at the Christian Science church. I was thinking of the Dharma talk I was giving tomorrow morning at ten.

We waded through ankle-deep snow on the sidewalk and stomped into the Fitzwilliam Inn where we were met by two ghouls. One ghoulish waitress said, "Sorry. We're fully booked."

"Where's the bathroom?" Bill asked.

Another ghoul/waitress said, "I'll call the Ashburn House. Maybe they have rooms." She was already dialing. "Hi, Carol. We have a couple here who need a room tonight. Unh-hunh. Unh-hunh. Okay.

"They've got a room for you," she said, turning her blackened eyes to us. "It's just three houses up. You can have dinner here first."

Walking past a fireman and a go-go dancer at the bar, Bill and I settled at a table by the blazing fireplace. We thanked our unseen guardian angels and the seen angels, who were trying to trick us into believing they were demonic even though they were treating us warmly and kindly. Maybe I could be an angel for Halloween?

After a cozy dinner, we trudged back out into even deeper snow. We tried to drive the Prius uphill to the nearby Ashburn House, but the anti-skid device brought the car to a complete tire-spinning halt before we reached the B&B. We backed downhill and drove right back in to our convenient parking spot beside the sidewalk at the Fitzwilliam Inn.

We then got out my hiking poles and walked back uphill in nearly knee-deep snow. The steps to Ashburn House had not been shoveled, but Carol let us in, and, like dogs, we shook the snow off our heads and jackets.

A warm and dry house! A bedroom! We had no toothbrushes and no night clothes. I had no case to pop my contact lenses into, but we had a four-poster bed, and we had each other. We drifted off to sleep to the sound of a snowplow truck scraping the road just thirty feet in front our bedroom.

Sunday morning dawned clear. I looked out our bedroom window to a blanket of white and a plowed street with a thin glaze of icy snow. Hiking pole in hand, I opened the front door and stepped into hip-deep snow. Floundering through the front yard, I reached the street and quickly made my way back to the Fitzwilliam Inn. Every few minutes, another pickup with a snowplow drove by. I pushed the Prius's power button, so it could warm up while I wrestled two feet of snow off the windshield and rear window. When I could see through the windows, I tried to gun the car backwards. It went nowhere. I got out of the car and flagged down the next passing pickup truck with a snowplow. This angel-man scraped out the ten feet of snow between the Prius and the street, and Bill and I were ready to drive home so that we could each go to work.

We'd spent seven hours with the grandchildren and seventeen hours driving home. That's the price of love.

# The Kitchen Sponge

At least once a week, Bill holds one of his shirts up to my nose. "Smell this," he says.

I sniff and say, "I don't smell anything." The shirt remains under my nose so I sniff the armpit of the proffered T-shirt again. "Nothing," I confirm.

"Well, okay," he says. "I guess I'll wear it." But before he puts it on, he washes his armpits and re-applies deodorant.

Later in the afternoon, I go to the kitchen sink. "Bill," I say, "you have got to wash this sponge. Smell it. Yech." I tell him this because we have divided the kitchen tasks in half. I do the cooking; he does the washing up. So he's in charge of the sponge, the scrubby, the table mopping cloth, his favorite brush with a handle, and the dishwasher.

He sniffs. "I don't smell anything."

Without another word, I toss the sponge down the basement steps toward the washing machine. Why can't he get in the habit of running the sponge through the dishwasher? Or he could let the sponge soak in a cereal bowl of bleach water. A few days later, I toss the table-mopping cloth down the basement stairs because it feels slimy.

How can a man who is so sensitive to body odors not smell a kitchen sponge?

When his daughter visited for his 75th birthday, she brought the birthday cake and a brand-new sponge, which she conveniently left behind. She told him to throw his old sponge away.

"But Jeni," he says. "You can clean a sponge by soaking it in bleach water." When I hear my words coming out of Bill's mouth, I know he's actually heard the message I've delivered dozens of times. Now he's taking on the parental role with his adult child, delivering a message that she probably doesn't appreciate any more than he does.

Jeni's a professional woman with young children. She doesn't have time to soak a dirty sponge in bleach water. She just throws the offender away and buys what she needs.

But ever since then, Bill has been assiduous about cleaning the kitchen sponge. Sometimes he runs it through the dishwasher. Sometimes he soaks it in bleach water. Sometimes the cleaning woman can't stand it and throws his old sponge into her cleaning bucket while she breaks a new blue sponge out of its cellophane wrapper and places it at the kitchen sink.

## Bill's Computers

Down in our basement sits Bill's first computer—a 1983 Sharp luggable. About the size and weight of a sewing machine, it was revolutionary when it came out. Bill was selling insurance at the time and used it to run certain insurance programs and to write letters on WordStar.

He moved in with me in 1989 and for another two years continued to write letters on his Sharp computer to his wife's divorce attorney. A few years later, I offered him my 1987 IBM—the very first laptop—but he liked his luggable and stuck with it into the new millennium. In 1999 his journalist daughter set him up with a Yahoo e-mail account that he checked every month or so on my computer, since his seventeen-year-old Sharp, which ran five-and-a-quarter-inch floppy diskettes, could not connect to the new Internet.

Early in this century, I began buying laptops every couple of years. The HP was too big, so I gave it to his daughter Lauren, who has been in college since 2004. Since she has Asperger's, and the employment outlook is dismal for anyone on the autism spectrum, she may just stay in college for several more years.

The somewhat smaller Dell laptop was also too big, so I left it with Lauren two years later. Now I have an Acer that I like well enough, and Bill has claimed it as his. In 2007, he took a major step and did his taxes with TurboTax.

So Bill can type a letter—hunt and peck. He can check his e-mail—about every three weeks. He can file his taxes. And he does online banking with ING. Several months ago he bought a printer for the laptop, so he can now print out whatever he wants—sometimes.

When he wants to order tickets for the New England Youth Theater, I tell him, "Go online." He'd rather call, but then he gets the message that the box office doesn't open until noon. He wants to go to the Christmas Revels at the Hopkins Center at Dartmouth. "Go online," I tell him.

"I don't know how," he says. "I don't know how to use Google."

"Here," I say, handing him my iPad. I type in "The Hop, Dartmouth."

"Now what do I do?" he asks.

I touch Christmas Revels, and hand it back to him.

"Can't you just tell me what to do?" he asks.

"Experiment," I say.

"Cheryl. Just tell me."

"You're not going to break anything," I say. "Just try."

He pokes the screen and harrumphs. "Oh no! What did I do?" He tries to hand the iPad back to me.

"Here," I say, touching the screen. "Choose your seats."

Through seventy years on the piano, Bill has tried to not play a wrong note so that he won't learn or practice a bad habit. In exactly the same way, he's trying not to hit any wrong keys on the computer, but it's a whole different keyboard. On the computer, success is going from failure to failure without losing enthusiasm.

# Honey Woman: A Ten-Minute Writing Exercise

*(In this exercise, the facilitator calls out a word every thirty seconds, which is then incorporated into the writing. The writers have no idea what the next word will be. The words called out this way are in boldface print.)*

"T**aste this honey**," he said. She stuck out her tongue and squeezed her eyes shut. She trusted him. He gazed at her adoringly, knowing her long and complicated **narrative**. He was undisturbed by her surface prickers, which were off-putting to others. He felt her to be soft as a **cotton** ball, and he trusted her to be herself.

Yes, sometimes they were **sore** at each other, but the **architecture** of their relationship was not **brittle**. She had done the groundwork early on, by insisting on the **vocabulary** of I-statements. She did not tolerate you-statements. It had taken years to train him, partly perhaps because she was short on **feminine** wiles.

But all along, he had been confident in the **silver** lining of her occasional storm clouds. He had had his share of relationships with **madness**, beginning with his mother. Now he had a **lush** and luscious woman, and he would **bend** in her direction. It was his pattern to be pliable, flexible. He had **tiptoe**d around those mad women, but this honey woman had something **childlike** about her that he could not **undo**. She relied on him **tender**ly until a storm shook them both. Then it passed just as suddenly.

He didn't **crumble**, but quietly held his own. Her tantrums could not **erode** his faith in her, for he was deeply faithful to this what-you-see-is-what-you-get woman.

## Do-It-Yourself

When I was 29, I wanted to be self-reliant. I wanted to do everything myself. That was the fall I moved into a cabin on Windmill Hill, half a mile beyond the end of the road.

The cabin had a woodstove and an outhouse. The running water ran all the time, since it came from a gravity-fed spring. In fact, the water *had* to run constantly; otherwise it would freeze in the 200-yard-long PVC pipe that ran over the ground from a spring in the woods to the house. Cold and clear, the water ran out of the faucet and into the old porcelain double sink that had come from a salvage yard, and then down the drain and into the open air, where it tinkled back into the earth.

The house sat about three feet above the ground on concrete sonotube posts, so in the fall I'd stack bales of hay or bags of leaves around the base as insulation. Otherwise the winter winds would blow under the house and up through the floorboards. This owner-built house had been constructed as an envelope around the post and beams, so when the wind did blow—as it certainly could up there on *Wind*mill Hill—I was sure the house would just twist into a pile of sticks.

Every fall I stapled plastic onto the single-pane salvaged windows. On Town Meeting Day in early March, I planted seeds in flats until the be-windowed south-facing kitchen counters were covered. That summer, when I was thirty, I had my very own garden for the first time.

When I moved into the cabin I immediately ditched the propane refrigerator in favor of a twenty-year-old Norge that cost me $25 and lasted another twenty years before I regretfully allowed it to be picked up by Efficiency Vermont, which gave me $50 for it. Now *that* was a dependable fridge.

After the first snowfall in November, I could no longer drive downhill to the cabin because my 1973 rear-wheel-drive red Chevy Nova could not negotiate the turn-uphill-turn driveway, even with snow tires. From Thanksgiving until mud season dried up, sometime around Tax Day, I parked my car at the end of the town road and carried my groceries in and my laundry out to a laundromat.

My neighbors—the reason I had moved into this hollow in the first place—had two small children and a Willys jeep that plowed the perilous driveway. They drove; I walked.

I dreamed of friends coming to visit me in this house thirty minutes from town and inaccessible five months of the year. My new dream analyst pointed out just how unavailable I was making myself at a time of life when I said I wanted a relationship.

The sex I had in that house was with a married man who drove an hour and a half for occasional afternoons. Realizing there was no future in this relationship, I let it go and swung into a fling with another married man. Then I found a premature ejaculator who was still in love with his ex-girlfriend. I was never happy with the self-reliance of sleeping single.

I stoked the stove in the morning before I walked up the hill to my car in the beautiful lavender-and-peach midwinter dawns at 7:15 a.m. After the ten-minute walk, I drove the 35 minutes into town to my job at the Council on Aging where I coordinated health programs for the elderly. After work I couldn't really stay in Brattleboro to meet a friend or go to a movie because I needed to go home and stoke the woodstove again.

I bought five cord of wood to keep me warm that winter when it was twenty degrees below zero for two weeks straight. Fortunately, my mother sent me a chamber pot for Christmas. Think about it: an outhouse in the dark at twenty below.

When my parents came to visit in the fall, my dad bought me a Homelite chain saw. But I was too scared to use it so I ordered more cords of wood for the winter and stacked it near the makeshift front door.

Around this time, I decided I was tired of renting and was ready to build my own house; I asked my dad to help me financially, since I was saving nothing on my $8,000-a-year salary.

Ten years after graduating from college with a math degree, and five years after earning a master's degree in International Administration, I still had never earned even $10,000 a year.

I thought I would design my own house, so I took a continuing education class with David Howard at Keene State College, where I came up with a house plan. I gave the plan to a builder friend of a friend, and he turned my squares of paper into artwork. (He had a degree in sculpture.)

Wanting to do things myself, I bought a little Mazda

truck and tried to figure out how to make it a four-wheel-drive. But in 1978, four-wheel drive small trucks were still eight years in the future. So, again that winter, I had to park my truck at the end of the town road and walk in and out.

I thought I would build my own cabinets, so I took a continuing education woodworking class at the high school in Brattleboro. Six weeks later, my cabinet door wobbled, so I hired a finish carpenter to build cherry cabinets with black walnut handles.

I thought I would save money by buying doors from a salvage yard. It took me years to strip four of them, and I never did finish two of them. One I eventually painted. My bathroom door is still unfinished, 33 years later.

So many things I have tried to do-it-myself.

It has taken me decades to realize that do-it-yourself takes a lot of time and a lot of interest. It turns out I'm not that interested in woodworking. I'm interested in the *idea* of woodworking, and I staunchly believe that women should learn skills usually reserved for men, yet I haven't actually done it myself.

When I gave up my back-to-the-land persona in 1982, at the age of 34, I tried on a yuppie persona for a couple of years, but I still sewed my own linen or wool suits to wear to work. Then I gave up sewing my own clothes when clothes became cheap in the late 1980s.

I laid a stone patio and dug a little fish pond and laid a stone terrace around it. A few years later, I had a professional stone mason re-lay my patio and refurbish the little terrace around the tiny fish pond. The professional job looks so much better than my stone-laying job. The last relic of my handiwork was a tire retaining wall, which came down a year ago and has been replaced by a beautiful stone wall.

The last thing I gave up was doing my gardens myself. When my body started to complain at age 55, I hired a gardener. Now she does most of the heavy lifting, and I do most of the finger-pointing. "Here." "This." "That." "There."

I've reached the age when I'm ready to hire other people to do things for me. I am just not going to lay out a book or create an e-book by myself. The learning curve is too steep, and it is so much easier to let other people do it themselves.

# Cooperation

I'VE SPENT SO MUCH of my life trying to be self-reliant that I'm not very good at doing things with someone else. Bill, for instance.

But Bill loves to do things together. Like stack five cord of wood. Before I met Bill, I stacked five cord by myself every fall. Now that he's in charge of the wood, he needs to instruct me, and he corrects my wood stacking. Therefore, I disappear so he can't find me until he's done for the day.

At the end of May, he'll say, "Let's carry the ficus tree outdoors." I walk into the greenhouse, grab the five-foot-tall ficus at the base of its four intertwined trunks and heft it out the door and down the steps to the patio under the deck where all the houseplants have summer vacation. Bill chases after me with the saucer.

We used to carry my 45-pound kayak together in order to lift it onto the car rack and then strap both mine and Bill's to the top of the car. Bill has always preferred to carry his 25-pound kayak all by himself, since he feels that my reaching and lifting are not dependable. He doesn't want to strain his back with any sudden saves.

Then in June I went on a wildflower paddle in the Retreat Meadows. I watched Linda Hecker open the back of her white Subaru station wagon and drag out her kayak. The stern bumped over a gravel driveway down to a dock where she single-handedly put the kayak in the water.

Aha! I could drag *my* heavy kayak to the pickup truck, let down the tailgate, nose it into position, walk to the stern of the kayak, and push. Then I could lift the end of the kayak with one hand and slam the tailgate closed with the other, and before you knew it, I'd be off to the Putney Landing all by myself to simply drift on the Connecticut River for an hour before dinner.

On the second weekend of December, Bill and I bought our Christmas tree. I headed my checkbook to the checkout while Bill and the Christmas tree salesman carried the tree to the truck.

Once we arrived home, there was no escaping the upcoming teamwork. Bill did his prep work—saw, gloves, loppers and rubber mallet. I did my prep work—a choice of two Christmas tree stands, one regular and one large, at the ready.

Still outdoors, Bill sawed off the bottom of the tree and lopped off the bottom branches. Then he tried tapping the base onto the trunk with the rubber mallet.

"Okay," Bill said. "You take the bottom. I'll take the top. Let's stand it up in the holder."

I held the bottom, and the tree stand fell off.

"Well, that didn't work," Bill said. "You'll have to guide it into the stand."

I stood obediently, mutely at the ready. Then I held the base of the tree into the stand, while Bill walked the top of the tree to vertical.

"Keep holding," he said as he walked around to see if the tree was straight. He made minor adjustments while I was crouched down on the cold sidewalk, my face full of balsam fir.

"Okay," he said. "Now I'll hold while you start screwing."

I obeyed.

One more attempt, and the tree entered the house feet first. I set the stand down while taller Bill tipped the tree into an upright position.

Now that's teamwork.

# Report Card on Life

My report card in first grade had two possibilities: S for "satisfactory" or U for "unsatisfactory." White-haired Mrs. Akers couldn't help herself and gave an occasional S+ or S–. I never received a U, but I can't imagine a U+ or a U–. How could "unsatisfactory" be "unsatisfactory plus"? "Unsatisfactory minus" would be really, really bad.

Actually, there's a lot to be learned from grading our experience as either satisfactory or unsatisfactory. Pretty soon we might realize just how much dissatisfaction we actually do experience in the midst of our happy-enough lives. I don't mean to be pessimistic so much as realistic. Just grade your own experience of the past twenty-four hours.

Bill took me out for a romantic Valentine's dinner at Bella Note. Satisfactory plus. The Linguine Adriatico was quite satisfying. However, I've noticed that wheat makes me sleepy, so I nearly dozed on the way back home and went straight to bed at 9:15. That was unsatisfactory as far as romance is concerned.

Bill always loves conversation, but sometimes I have very little to say at dinner. He finds that unsatisfactory. So, to make a romantic evening, he designated the evening's topic as "Let's reminisce about our travels." We talked about our travels in 1990, '91, and '92, and by that time dinner was over. He was feeling very good about sharing and connecting; he finds that satisfactory. I find talking about the past somewhat unsatisfactory since I think that memories are just a dream (that we believe in). But I kept my little dissatisfaction to myself.

Because the thing that is satisfactory is having a companion, having an intimate relationship, and having a Valentine.

## Cold and Hot Sleeping

When I was in my thirties, I wore socks to bed in the winter, even though I slept in a room right above a very good woodstove. Socks and a flannel nightgown that my sister had made for me—white with tiny purple flowers in the ruffled style of the mid-1980s. I wore socks and a flannel nightgown, but I didn't have flannel sheets, so, for warmth, I stacked my pillow on my feet since I slept without a pillow.

I thought that sleeping without a pillow meant I wouldn't get a double chin, but that was just a myth I read in *Glamour* magazine when I was 19 and believed for thirty years. And I can tell you now: that idea was a total fabrication of some nameless and forgotten writer.

I cracked open the window beside my bed so I could have fresh air all night long. Most winter nights, I would bury my head under the blankets and then create a little air hole for my nostrils, so I could breathe in the cool night air.

My grandmother died in November 1987, a month before I turned forty, so I took her pansy flannel sheet with matching pansy percale fitted sheet and matching pansy pillowcases. I also took her red woolen blanket and two afghans that she had made—one crocheted in a cartwheel pattern and one knitted in stripes of various pinks. The flannel, the wool, and Nonnie's crocheted love kept me warmer on winter nights.

The following fall, I met Bill, and mail-ordered a long-sleeved blue silk pajama top from Silks Plus. Yes, sleeping with someone else kept me warm.

When Bill moved his queen-sized bed to my house the following summer, I mail-ordered flannel sheets for toasty sleeping all through the winters of my forties.

Then the too-hot sleeping of my fifties caused me to doff all sleeping attire from April to November. For the coldest quarter of the year, December through March, I wore an oversized T-shirt to bed. "Oversized" was "in" in the 1990s. I never really liked T-shirts, but I would occasionally receive one as a gift—a gardening T-shirt or a solstice T-shirt that I never wore outside the winter bed.

Now, in my sixties, I enjoy a sheer nightie even when the weather is cold. I'm thankful for the snuggleness of my companion for as long as I have him, because when the deep winter of my life comes, I'll revert to stacking pillows along my back and feet while my double chin vibrates from my fitful snores on a Tempur-Pedic pillow.

# Best of the Blog 2012
## The Ten Supremes

Generosity
Integrity
Renunciation
Wisdom
Energy
Patience
Truthfulness
Resolve
Loving-Kindness
Equanimity

www.themeditativegardener.blogspot.com

## Growing New Roots

Cold temperatures are keeping me indoors now that winter has truly arrived. Zero degrees this morning holds a few inches of snow on the ground, and the fishpond is well and truly frozen.

The only gardening available to me is my houseplants, so I water them and pick off dead leaves. I give several of them a haircut—begonias, geraniums, and wandering Jew—and place the cuttings in jars of water so they'll root.

What would you like to root in this new year? Self-compassion? Joy? Being of service? Friendliness? Patience?

In order to root these (or any other) beneficial qualities into our daily life, we have to grow new routes for our mind to take. And there's no better place to begin than with ourselves. Send well-wishes to yourself right now.

*May I feel safe.* (Feel around inside your body. Does someplace "feel" safe? After a couple of seconds, move on.)

*May I feel happy.* (Does someplace in your body "feel" happy?)

*May I feel healthy.*

*May I feel peaceful.* (Does your big toe "feel" peaceful?)

Repeat these phrases and allow them to gradually percolate into your mind and into your body. By the time my cuttings have rooted, you will have established some new neuronal routes yourself.

# Tapping into Happiness

With daytime temperatures above freezing and nighttime temperatures below freezing, the sap is starting to run. It's time to tap the sugar maples.

My Dharma friend, Vera, tapped 22 trees in her yard in mid-February. My farmer-neighbor taps 147 trees on my property while he himself has thousands of taps. It takes forty gallons of sap to boil down to one luscious golden gallon of maple syrup.

Sometimes, it feels like it takes forty years of life to distill ourselves into the person we want to be, but haven't quite dared.

My life began at forty when I followed my bliss and wrote a book. For my friend Trudy, life began at sixty when she left an abusive marriage.

Do we just let dissatisfaction boil our lives away? How do we finally tap into sweet happiness?

There are two kinds of happiness:

- Surface Happiness—when we get what we want, and
- the Deep Happiness of contentment with life, regardless of our outer circumstances.

The first step to finding deep happiness is to practice gratitude every day. Notice, really notice the people, things, and situations in your life for which you are truly grateful.

Sweet.

## Proliferating Spider Plant

March is the time to clip all the "spiders" off my prolific spider plant and root them in a jar of water. They root so easily. Then, in May, I use the little plants as an edging in my white garden.

Yes, we usually think that a spider plant is a houseplant that belongs in a hanging basket, but why not use it as an annual in the flowerbed? What fun to see an old friend in a new place! And all that edging is free.

As we become more familiar with joy, and how it naturally arises from a lack of desire, we find that joy proliferates and we can "plant" it all over our life.

Time to take cuttings of the spider plant so it can proliferate.

## Manna in the Garden

Ten yards of mulch was delivered in mid-April. Every year I order a special "Manna Mix," which is half-compost and half-mulch.

Manna, which fell from heaven, fed the wandering Israelites in the desert for forty years (Exodus 16:14–36). More prosaically, this manna mix feeds my flowerbeds, which in turn, delight my eyes and pleasure my mind.

What feeds us spiritually? A bit of quiet time, a moment of solitude, a stroll through our garden. Bringing mindfulness to this moment relaxes the body and relaxes the mind.

When we let down our guard, as we can safely do in the garden, we can relax into our authentic self. We come home to ourselves and are sustained by the manna of our garden.

## Cold Wind

A cold front blew in its strong winds one day in late April, and tore last year's tan beech leaves off the trees. The wind raked leaves across the lawn and into the woods, then changed its mind, switched directions, and blew them across the lawn to the other side. The air was thick with flying dead leaves.

Sometimes our cold heart rakes old, dead wrongs back and forth across our mind. The winds of blame and pain blow strong, and it seems we are at the mercy of our changeable mind.

Stop.
Don't blame the trigger.
Let go.
Substitute the opposite.
Loving-kindness warms the heart and cools the mind.

Stopping the mind from the rampage of the cold front is a hard assignment. We may want to present our cold aloofness to the world with an unfeeling "Whatever."

Dare to feel that unpleasant, oh-so-uncomfortable emotion.

Find the sensation in the body.

Name the emotion if you can, but if you can't, don't worry.

Sink into the ouchy sensation.

Press into it like an acupressure point.

Watch the mind/pain let go of its own accord.

Apply the balm of loving-kindness.

# Amaryllis Patience

An amaryllis is blooming in my solarium. I bought this pot of two bulbs at a library plant sale. I've been watering their strappy green leaves for almost two years, and—finally! Flowers!

Sometimes, even though we consistently water our meditation practice, we feel like nothing is happening.

Patience, my dear friend.
Patience with your meditation.
Patience with your nearest and dearest.
Patience with your aging parents and with your co-workers.

Patience is one of the ten supreme qualities (*paramis* or *paramitas*) that we practice, practice, practice. After all, practice makes perfect.

Patience is an antidote to irritation. "Count to ten," your mother said. Nowadays, you might count ten breaths before you respond.

Patience is an antidote to desire.
Watch desire arise in the mind. Feel "I want" in your body. Notice that it passes.

Even if the same desire reappears in your mind one-half second later.

Patience is an antidote to confusion.

You don't actually need to know the answer to the question right this minute (although you may *want* the answer *right now*).

Feel confusion in your body.

Watch the ripples of confusion in your mind.

Patience is a remedy that cures many ills, many dis-eases of the mind.

Patience, my dear. It has taken the amaryllis two years to bloom.

# Short-Lived Redbud

Several years ago I brought home a gallon of redbud seeds from the woods near the house I grew up in, in Indiana. Redbuds (*Cercis canadensis*) are a delightful little spring-blooming tree, whose pinky-red "buds" are followed by heart-shaped leaves.

I now live on the northernmost edge of the range of redbud, so I planted my little seedlings in the sunniest location I have, on the edge of the woods, facing south. One of these redbuds now overarches a third of my herb garden. And it will soon fall victim to the new construction of a garage.

Something dear and delightful is going to die—very soon. Everything we cherish will perish.

We could take the attitude "Eat, drink, and be merry for tomorrow we will die," but this intemperateness trades desperation for momentary pleasure.

Seeing clearly the desperation of our situation, we could instead feel grateful for what we do have. Gratitude leads to joy, and joy feels like love.

I love my redbud tree.

# Honesty

Now that the daffodils are finishing blooming, tulips usually take up the slack. But I gave up planting tulips years ago because I was tired of waging war on bulb-eating chipmunks. I so much more enjoy watching chippies scamper around the flower beds than growling at them for their culinary predilections.

Money plant (*Lunaria*) and summer snowflake (*Leucojum*) are blooming all over my garden now. They have been flowering for three weeks and will continue for another three weeks. I do like flowers that last a long time.

Money plant is also called *honesty*. This concept of honesty leads us directly to two of the five precepts:

1. Not taking what isn't offered.
2. Speaking truthfully and helpfully.

Honesty, or truth-telling, needs to be balanced with being beneficial. What we are about to say may well be true, but is it helpful?

The Metta Sutta (the sutra on loving-kindness) says that one aspect of developing the skill of goodness is to be "straightforward and gentle in speech." Honesty, or truth-telling, needs to be balanced with being beneficial. What we are about to say may well be true, but is it helpful?

Sometimes we refrain from honesty in order not to hurt the other person's feelings. This intention is a very fine line to walk, so I frequently reflect on how "straight-forward and gentle" applies to my current situation. We don't sacrifice honesty for gentleness nor do we sacrifice gentleness for truth.

Honesty "holds" the bloom in my garden during this mid-spring season. I work on holding the bloom of honesty in all my relationships.

## Bluebird of Happiness

I have installed several bluebird houses out near my vegetable garden because that's the most open area I have here in the woods. You're supposed to put two houses within ten feet of each other, so the swallows can have one and the bluebirds the other. Otherwise, the swallows will take over a single house and defend their territory.

I bolt the bluebird house to an eight-foot-long PVC pipe, then slide the pipe down over a fencepost, like a sleeve. Usually chickadees take up residence, or sometimes a mouse family.

In May, I saw an actual bluebird on one fencepost and two swallows on two other fence posts. What a festival of blue and bluish birds! I was thrilled to see the bluebird of happiness. And I was equally thrilled to have a rare (for me) sighting of sleek swallows.

Thrill. Joy. Happiness. Really, any bird can touch the happiness chord in us. Stop. Feel what happiness feels like. Allow it to permeate your body. Soak in happiness for at least thirty seconds—this "soaking" will retrain your brain so that you'll have easier access to happiness next time.

> *Somewhere over the rainbow,*
> *Bluebirds fly.*

Our hearts can fly over the rainbow too.

## Simplify Your Flowerbed

My theory of flowerbeds is to plant small clumps near the house, which can become larger the farther you go away from the house. Near the house, a clump of flowers can be about a foot in diameter; farther away, two to three feet in diameter.

In practice this means ongoing division and taking "spreaders" (such as bee balm or phlox) out of the neat little beds altogether. It all depends on your tolerance for dividing. Some gardeners can't bear to divide their clumps at all.

Flowers can overwhelm our little gardens, stuff can overwhelm our house, and multitasking can overwhelm our lives. Simplify your garden, your house, and your to-do list. Create some breathing space for your plants and yourself.

What one thing can you let go of today?

## Generosity Cancels Greed

The library has a Book & Plant Sale on Memorial Day weekend. What a great opportunity to give them a pile of books I am not going to read again. And it's also an excellent opportunity for me to stroll through the garden, trowel in hand, and dig up plants that are too crowded or that have volunteered in the "wrong" place. In the vegetable garden, I have four square feet of dill that reseeded itself. That's a *lot* of dill. I pot it up into two flats of six-packs.

Generosity, giving things away, cancels out greed. I used to collect books. I thought more books was good. Then I took a hard look at my wall of books. It really wasn't very pretty. Is that what I thought my brain looked like?

I used to collect plants, and, after thirty years of adding plants and plants naturally spreading, my flowerbeds are full to overflowing. In order to put something in, I have to take something—or a few somethings—out.

Let's take several things out of the flower and vegetable gardens and give them away. Let them multiply in someone else's garden, and the joy of giving will multiply in our heart.

# Caught Red-Handed in the Red Cabbage

While I'm in the vegetable garden, I see a dark shadow dart near my new red cabbage plants. I freeze. A vole peeks out from under a nearby foxglove's skirt of velvety leaves, dashes through the fence, and grabs the lowest leaf off the red cabbage. It drags the palm-sized leaf through the fence back to its hiding place. I hope that's enough for breakfast, lunch, and dinner.

A nearby cabbage has seven leaves. The plant that the vole is de-limbing has three leaves remaining.

I feel generous. I'm not going to eat those lower leaves. The vole raider can have it, as long as it leaves the stem for me. How high can a vole reach anyway?

Maybe that's the strategy: Buy plants that are taller than five-inch-long voles.

The Buddha says:

> With one's wealth collected justly,
> won through one's own efforts,
> one shares both food and drink
> with beings who are in need.

I am rich in cabbage and broccoli plants. And I am sharing my food with a vole-being who needs to feed her babies.

# Voles 30, Cheryl 6

Okay. The voles win. They have scored more of my three-inch broccoli seedlings than I have. Nibbled off at the stem. And in the game of cabbages, it's: Voles 12, Cheryl 0. My little cabbage seedlings have completely disappeared, even the four six-inch red cabbage seedlings that I bought at a farm stand.

I'm going to the farmers' market to buy six-packs of broccoli, green cabbage, red cabbage, and, while I'm at it, Brussels sprouts. I want those muscular ten-inch-tall plants so that a vole will need a chainsaw if she's going to cut down a broccoli tree.

Voles are quick, dark, gerbil-sized creatures that look like a shadow as they dart through the Swiss chard, which they have also nibbled to the nubbins.

A fellow master gardener has made several vol-inators: he covers a little wooden Clementine box with bark to make it look like a burrow, but he furnishes it with mousetraps inside.

I just cannot do it. Every morning I take a vow to not harm creatures. I guess this includes the team of voles living around my garden. I'd rather feed the voles my entire crop of cabbage.

But I do have a strategy for our game next season. . . .

# The Honor System

A nearby farmer loaded 26 bales of mulch hay onto my Toyota Tacoma pickup truck. Wow! She really knows how to stack hay! She did this while she was milking her five sweet brown Jersey cows. Every Monday, I pick up a half gallon of raw milk from her farm. While I'm there, I may get a dozen eggs, a pound of butter, or some cream for whipping. It's all stored in a refrigerator along with a cash box in a tiny shed, so I can go there any time of the day or night. Everyone pays on the honor system.

If you look closely, you see that we all depend on the honor system. The vast majority of our interpersonal transactions with each other are indeed honorable. We don't take what isn't freely offered. We pay our share.

We feel right when we do the right thing, when we act honorably. Our conscience bothers us when we act dishonorably. We may dismiss our little cheat with a shrug of the shoulders, and think, "They'll never notice." But *we* notice. We know of our own dishonesty. We are our own judges. We charge ourselves with dishonorable conduct. No one else may ever judge us for that little, tiny cheat. But if you were dying a few hours later, would you feel absolved? Or would you feel regret and remorse?

Acting honorably puts our mind at ease.

# Giving and Its Unseen Strings

The last two ninety-degree days brought breezes with them and gave us the delightful treat of hot and cool at the same time. Breezes blowing through open windows felt delightful in the meditation hall. One *sangha* volunteer brought a bouquet of flowers for the visiting nun who was leading the meditation and teaching. Later, another meditator quietly moved the bouquet to the anteroom, due to chemical sensitivities.

How do you feel when your act of generosity is not accepted? Perhaps you offer something and the recipient says, "No thanks." Or perhaps they accept, but don't put your gift in a place of honor (such as the flowers being placed in the meditation hall). Or perhaps they accept, but then later pass the gift on to someone else.

These are all opportunities to look at our intentions. Ostensibly, we thought we were being generous. But then we see/feel the strings we had perhaps unknowingly attached to our gift.

We want the recipient to be happy or grateful or surprised. Or we want them to like us or love us. Maybe we just want them to think well of us. But maybe they'll think ill of us for giving them something they consider to be useless or even ugly.

The road to hell, as well as the road to stress and distress, is paved with good intentions.

Let's be kind to ourselves. Let's give because we want to give. Period.

How the recipient responds is none of our business.

## More Tomatoes

Tomatoes! I've got 'em. I have the most abundant crop I've had in years. And yet I have fewer plants. Oh! That was hard—to *stop* buying tomato plants.

The cleaning lady gave me five sungolds—*the* best cherry tomatoes I've tasted. Two plants died, which left me with the perfect number of three. Sungolds sprawl, so three is quite sufficient. I also planted three grape (cherry) tomatoes. Because of their meatiness, I sun-dry the grape tomatoes so I can have the flavor-burst this winter. (I gave the rest of the six-pack to a friend.)

As usual, here in the North Country, I planted Jet Star, a small but early tomato, just to hedge my bets.

The cleaning lady gave me five Opalkas. (She plants only heirloom seeds.) A.k.a. the Polish Torpedo, these are *big* meaty paste tomatoes.

I bought a handful of other plants, and then I stopped.

Now six cherry tomatoes and eighteen other tomato plants may sound like a lot to you, but some years I squeeze in 36.

Knowing how much is too much, I restrained my impulse for *more* seedlings last spring. And yet, in August, I did have "more" tomatoes than usual.

# Transplanting Our Values

A local garden club is having a plant sale in late September—an idea I heartily approve. September and October are excellent months for gardening—a great time for dividing, transplanting, cleaning up the flowerbeds, and even working on a new garden project.

Meanwhile, garden tours have ceased, and some nurseries have already closed their garden gates—*Closed for the Season.*

Some of us are approaching the end of our working life, so how shall we divide and transplant the knowledge, wisdom, and skills we've acquired? Being generous with our time and our skills, perhaps volunteering to serve others, is a great way to transplant our values and intentions.

What's most important to you? How can you pass that along to another generation?

The Dharma is most important to me, and I'm teaching three classes this fall.

But now, I'm going out to the garden to dig perennials for the plant sale.

# Redecorating the Entrance to Your Home

Early October is the time to redecorate the front step. Time to bring the pots of annual flowers into the solarium and wonder how many will survive the cool dryness and the decreasing light. Time to replace the planters with pots of mums, flowering kale, or pumpkins and gourds.

While we're at it, we'd like to redecorate our personalities. Take that irksome characteristic of ours straight to the compost pile, and replace it with something bright and cheery and socially acceptable. Or maybe we'd just like to forget about it and wish it would go away all by itself.

If we are using our ego to strong-arm ourselves into a new mold, it isn't going to work. The ego has learned to survive as it is, thank you very much. Using one sub-personality to dislodge another sub-personality? They each have their own turf.

Instead, bring mindfulness to that unskillful aspect. Bring that "unfortunate" quality into your heart this winter, and simply be mindful of it each time it appears. Feel what irritation feels like in the body. Feel what the thought, "I'm so stupid" feels like. Notice confusion when it arises and feel the discomfort that comes with it.

Notice these traits or your own particular idiosyncrasies. Live with them, really live with them for the next month or two as if they were unruly puppies.

Practice this loving-kindness meditation toward yourself:

> I love myself as I am, angry.
>
> I love myself as I am, confused.
>
> I love myself as I am, feeling stupid.

Use your own words.

Be kind to yourself.

# Plant Garlic Now

October is the time to plant garlic. It needs about six weeks to establish its root system before the ground freezes, but before it has an opportunity sprout green.

Choose the largest heads from this year's garlic crop. This is the hard part. Those best, fattest cloves are going into the ground, not into a soup or spaghetti sauce, nor into the oven for roasting. Let the best go in order to multiply and become next year's crop.

Wouldn't we rather keep the best for ourselves and give away our ratty-tatty stuff? Wouldn't we rather keep the new and give our used stuff to a thrift store or the church rummage sale?

The highest form of generosity is *raja* (think: *maharaja*), or kingly giving. Queenly giving gives openhandedly, openheartedly, and even without letting anyone know where the gift comes from.

In the case of garlic, we are giving to ourselves. Choose the best cloves, plant them, and harvest a king's ransom of garlic next July.

# A Clump of Bulbs

When I dug plants out of the white garden to save them from the trenching, I found a big clump of daffodils, already sprouted and ready to keep on growing. This "find" provides the perfect opportunity to divide the overcrowded clump of bulbs and even give some of them away.

Our lives become overcrowded with busy-ness. One activity spawns another. Every new material item requires some sort of maintenance, such as dusting or washing or finding a place to store the darn thing. Things pile up on top of each other. Responsibilities proliferate.

It's time to divide those responsibilities. Give items away. Hand over responsibility to someone else (even though this is very hard.)

After a period of rest this winter, you too will bloom.

## Forcing Hyacinths

In late November, I force hyacinths. The naked bulbs sit in their vases, suspended above water. They sit there in the dark cool basement for three months or so before the flowers begin to sprout and unfurl.

In our lives, we sometimes force ourselves to be nice because we think that being nice is the same as being good. But goodness is a skill that we can develop. The instructions are in the beginning lines of the Metta Sutta.

> *This is what is to be done*
> *by one who is skilled in goodness,*
> *and who seeks the path of peace.*
>
> *Let them be able and upright,*
> *straightforward and gentle in speech,*
> *humble and not conceited,*
> *contented and easily satisfied,*
> *unburdened by duties and frugal in their ways,*
> *peaceful and calm and wise and skillful,*
> *not proud and demanding in nature.*
>
> *Let them not do the slightest thing*
> *that the wise would later reprove.*

Consider pondering one of these pairs of skills at the end of your meditation. A "nice" person might be gentle in speech, but not "straightforward." How in the world can we do both? How can we say "No" (or even "No!") with an open heart?

Allow these phrases to grow in the dark of your subconscious. Some day you will be surprised by their blooming!

## Vase Collecting

Prior to beginning to force hyacinths in November, I collect forcing vases. In the past, I have bought a case of special forcing vases, but in the name of economy (and recycling), I now use secondhand, narrow-necked vases.

I love to go shopping at our local thrift store, called Experienced Goods, because, in addition to having a good selection of merchandise, all proceeds support our local hospice. Another good place to find vases is at the recycling center at our landfill. Called the Swap Program, it's open on Saturday mornings. Its mission is to keep stuff out of the landfill, and it figures that it succeeds to the tune of twenty tons a year. That's a lot of vases, flowerpots, and old skis. I take in items that are too decrepit for the thrift store, but still have some usability left in them.

I love the Swap Program because I take in junk, and I walk out with treasures that are free! I can't believe my great good luck. I pick one or two narrow-necked vases off the shelf and walk out, scot-free. Amazing!

This "reduce, reuse, recycle" business is not only fun and free, it also enables us to practice the qualities of generosity and renunciation. We give things to the thrift store (and receive a receipt to use for our itemized deductions on our taxes). My local thrift store supports a very good cause, hospice. It's a win-win situation. And, if we take on recycling as a spiritual practice, it becomes a win-win-win situation.

About half of my hyacinth forcing vases were free, and I can freely give them away, filled with a blooming hyacinth and a breath of spring.

## Little White Stars

My jade plant blooms with little white stars in late November. While this may not be unusual for people (and jade plants) living in zone 9 or 10, my jade plant and I live in zone 5. I didn't even know that a jade plant *could* bloom indoors until I accidentally discovered the secret: withhold water in September and October and the jade will bloom in November.

Actually, I don't have the heart to totally withhold water, so I water very, very lightly, just a couple of tablespoons of water once or twice a week.

Renunciation can make us bloom, too. It's counterintuitive. By giving up something, we will have more time, more energy, and quite possibly, more calm. In this season of buying more (buying more than we can really afford?), what would you be willing to give up? One trip to the store? Overeating at one meal? Turning off the computer an hour or two before bedtime?

Let's go outdoors and watch the stars shine in the night sky.

# "Been There, Done That": An Enemy of Gratitude

The barred owl called for several minutes as I was meditating at four o'clock this morning. "Who cooks for you? Who cooks for you all?" it asks.

My Thanksgiving cooking took a different form this year as I prepared some baked goods for the interludes between the forty-minute sits at seven, eight, nine, and ten o'clock at Vermont Insight on Thanksgiving morning. The cranberry-walnut scones were a big hit, but the kale-apple muffins were the big surprise.

During our final sit, I led a guided gratitude meditation:

> *Begin by practicing gratitude for all the ordinary, everyday things you take for granted:*
>
> *Running water, electricity, your car, a warm home, safety as you walk on the street;*
>
> *All the services: the post office, the bank and the magic of plastic, which so eases our lives.*
>
> *You can think of many more.*

Taking things for granted not only kills surprise in our lives, it numbs our delight in life. "Been there, done that" is an enemy of gratitude.

I can see I need to practice feeling surprise at kale. Wow! You can chop it up in your food processor and put it in muffins and the kale taste disappears. Magic!

# Baby Bok Choy-lets

Small baby bok choy are growing in the November garden. While I wasn't looking, two or three went to seed, and now bok choy-lets are growing along the seed stalk, which has fallen over and is lying (and rooting?) on the ground in a raised bed.

When we grow sweet little qualities in our inner garden—friendliness, kindness, cheerfulness, self-compassion—we sometimes aren't paying attention when they go to seed and multiply. Then someone says, "You are so grateful for the blessings of your life."

Hmmm. Well, yes, I am. I am practicing taking no-thing for granted—not my sweetie, not my life, and not my checking account. They are here today, but that doesn't mean they will be here tomorrow. Sometimes, change happens very fast. For now, change is happening slowly, and I can pretend that my sweetie and I will grow old together and be comfortable in our retirement.

But, some day, we ourselves will go to seed. When we are lying on our hospital bed, what will we harvest? Complaining or kindness? Meanness or mindfulness?

Let's root sweet qualities, beginning today.

# Abundance of Watercress

I pick watercress in early December. In two minutes, I fill up a five-gallon bucket.

Now for the sorting. I pinch off the top one-third of green leaves on stems and compost the remaining stem and yellowing leaves. I am separating green from yellow, separating a preponderance of leaves from the stem, which happily roots on any damp surface.

The Buddha suggests we separate wholesome from unwholesome. Just for today, imagine you are putting your skillful thoughts, words, and actions in one bucket, and your unskillful thoughts, words, and actions in another bucket.

Uh-uh-uh. No fair beating yourself up for *having* unskillful/unwholesome thoughts and actions. We are playing the part of an impartial observer here. *Oh! Isn't that interesting?* We are acting as a referee and calling the move "fair" or "foul" from a balanced viewpoint. Apply the scientific method; be curious. *How did that happen?* What happened just before that unwholesome/unskillful thought, word, or action appeared?

Meanwhile, I have about three gallons of watercress stems to go into the compost. This quantity of green being added to the mostly brown (at this time of year) compost will hurry the composting process along. The green and the brown teams work together to make rich and balanced soil.

When we stop judging our unskillful words and actions, we become more equanimous and calm because we are not taking the side of either team. We simply notice what's growing in our inner garden and call it *skillful* or *unskillful*. We call it as we see it, and let nature take its course. In the end, it's all compost for growing new habits.

## More from the Winter Garden

When it was fifty degrees in mid-December, I went to my community garden plot and pulled a few turnips. I also harvested the last three stalks of Brussels sprouts. And I cut my only flowering cabbage as a flower arrangement. Really! Isn't it amazing that the winter garden continues to feed and delight me!

Some of my friends signed up for a share of a winter CSA (community-supported agriculture) and are receiving biweekly bags of fresh winter veggies. Although the pickin's are slim in the winter garden, I find I am subsisting easily on what I find out there. If I go look, there is enough for the next meal. Fresh. Really, really local. And no oil is used to transport the vegetables or the vegetable-buyer (me).

One line from the Loving-Kindness (Metta) Sutta suggests that we practice being "contented and easily satisfied. . . ."

I am content with the offering of the winter garden and very well satisfied with a turnip-onion-garlic stew and some braised Brussels sprouts.

# At Home

# My iPhone Is My Bible

"My iPhone is my Bible," I overheard someone say. Really? All the information we need for living an intelligent life with integrity is on our smartphone?

There's Insight Timer, my meditation timer. I use Insight Timer almost every day that I'm home. If I want to, I can look to see who else in the world is meditating at the same time I am, and how long they are sitting for. Most people meditate for between five and fifteen minutes. I'm doing another commit-to-sit two hours every day with a couple of e-mail friends, so I set my timer for an hour every morning. I can choose any of six bells and whether or not I want a starting bell and whether or not I want the ending bell to ring with one or three chimes.

I also have Kindle on my iPhone, and I've downloaded the *Majjhima Nikaya—the Middle-Length Discourses of the Buddha*. My hard copy of the book is two inches thick. (I know this because I measured it with the Ruler app on my iPhone.) Much, much easier to look at my iPhone screen than to haul around any one of the five tomes of Buddhist scriptures. (The Buddha gave a *lot* of sermons in 45 years!)

The other apps on my iPhone are all about sense desire. Sense desire is one of the five hindrances to meditation, and to our spiritual life in general. Oh, I've got a pile of sense desires. A British meditation teacher jokes that mobile phones are the sixth hindrance.

Accuweather tells me the weather of wherever I am and wherever I'm going. Now I can dress (or undress) in sufficient and appropriate layers.

Mapquest tells me where in the world I am and how I can get to wherever I want to go. It uses a lot of battery power, but I have to say it is extremely handy for figuring out how to escape Heathrow in a rental car at ten at night. It's also handy for finding one of those gas stations that suddenly seem so elusive when you're returning a rental car to an airport.

I do love to know where I am and where I'm going. Where's a hotel? A restaurant? The map app tells all. Plus it's backlit so aging eyes can see it in the car at night, and you can pinch the map open so that aging eyes can actually read the name of the next street. I still carry maps around in my car, but I haven't looked at one in months.

I also love the handiness of my calendar on my iPhone. Only eight years ago, I carried four metal boxes in my purse—a cell phone, a camera, a GPS, and a personal organizer for my calendar and for keeping lists. Now I have one even-smaller metal box, and it's my favorite color—bright blue.

I have a To-Do list app on my iPhone. One of my meditation teachers doesn't even keep a to-do list. After digesting that information for three years, I've started taking my own to-do lists much less seriously. In fact, I now label the list "Sense Desires List" because the mind is really just making up stories about the person I want to be—organized, helpful, smart, and with a good (apparently bright blue) memory.

Being a self-taught naturalist, I have apps for the outdoors—Star Walk tells me the names of stars in the sky; the Moon Phase app tells me the status of the moon and when the next full moon is; iBirdPro tells me the names and calls of birds. Leaf Snap shows me which tree is which.

I have a batch of hiking apps. Accuterra shows me maps of hiking trails; the Compass app tells me which direction I'm going; and the Altimeter tells me how high I am. The Flashlight app lights my way at night.

For a trip to Mexico last year, I downloaded an English-Spanish dictionary. And for our London theatre tour this year, I downloaded a Shakespeare app with the complete works of Shakespeare, all his plays, word for word.

Now I can even use my iPhone to run credit cards because I hope other people have the sense desire to buy my book, *The Meditative Gardener*.

I have more apps—of course—but you see what I mean. With all these sense desires leading me on, who has time for a spiritual path? We can download the Bible onto our iPhones, but when can we find time to actually read it?

# Jewel Tones

JEWEL TONES ARE IN fashion again—royal blue, teal, bright pink, purples. I've been waiting twenty years for them to come back, so I'm buying clothes now for the next twenty years.

How do I know it's been twenty years? I bought turquoise, purple, and bright pink pants in 1986. I bought a pair of bright blue paints at J. C. Penney's in Brattleboro in 1993 when I was just finishing my master's degree at Antioch. When classes became boring, I'd rearrange people in my mind according to the colors they were wearing, and fan them out around my imaginary circle in a rainbow.

Then black came in, and earth tones, and I scrounged through thrift stores to find my so-called winter colors. I've endured more years of pastels, muddy colors, red and black, peach and turquoise than I care to remember. Jewel tones have been gone so long, women don't have any left in their closets to give to our local thrift store, Experienced Goods. The pickings there have been extremely thin for the past five years. Last summer I found some Guatemala pants in purple and blue stripes with thin stripes of turquoise and black. I thoughtlessly wear them here in Vermont, but on the airplane or anywhere else in this country, they scream, *Granola! This woman is a granola-head!*

Hey! I love granola. I make my own. It keeps me regular.

I just returned from northern Idaho, former home of

the Aryan Brotherhood, where I saw many Ron Paul signs in front yards. My sister took me shopping at the home store of Coldwater Creek. Her niece-in-law works for Coldwater Creek and has a 40 percent discount.

We walked into the store: jewel tones sparkled on the racks. Three-quarter-length sleeves, which I adore; I wear them in September and October and April through June. I bought four shirts.

I bought one bright-blue long-sleeved shirt with a jacket front attached. The faux jacket drapes nicely over my belly. But I can also tie the draping bit to accentuate my waist, which, while not as narrow as it used to be, is still one of my selling points. OMG, clothes that actually look good on me. Didn't Isabel Allende say something about accenting your good points, and hiding your unstylish bits? I love it that clothes are now actually supposed to fit. I'm not buying any more of that oversized stuff that makes me look like a little girl in dress-ups.

Jewel tones. Clothes that fit, that accent my feminine bodice and waist and hide my pendulous belly. Sign me up for the Coldwater Creek daily e-newsletter. Well, on second thought, that's way too much clutter in my e-mailbox. I've already unsubscribed from that idea.

I bought a pile of new clothes even though they were made in China, even though I prefer thrift stores.

I'm stocking up now, even though I know that in just a few years I will look hopelessly out of date, when jewel tones fade from fashion. Women will shake their heads at that eccentric old lady in purple who is wearing those oh-so-old clothes.

# Live It Loud

"Live it loud," Sarah says when I walk into writing group in a new bright-pink satin Chinese jacket. If the pink doesn't shock you, the satin sheen will shine you.

When I give directions to people coming to my house, I say, "The gray house wearing lipstick." Sort of like me—gray hair adorned with bright colors. The trim on my house is fuchsia, and that's just a foretaste of what you'll see when you walk in the front door—a teal living room next to a purple dining room.

Thirty years ago I started my walls off in Navajo White. Then after having my colors done, twenty years ago, I tried the icy colors: blue ice, pink ice, lavender ice, and gray ice. The walls still looked white.

Ten years ago, after both my parents died, I decided life was short. I didn't have time to wait for Tibetan colors to come into fashion. Besides, I'm not that fond of off-white.

I painted my office two tones of shocking pink. The teal living room has a swimming-pool-blue ceiling; the purple dining room has a lavender ceiling; and the adjoining kitchen has a pink ceiling. I love looking at the waves of sky-blue lilac pink on the ceilings.

So live it loud. No one is going to hear you anyway in the cacophony of busy-ness of today's world. You're just one more soundbite in the stream of audio input that everyone receives for hours every day.

You can play it safe and try to be acceptable. Do you think that will stop people from having opinions about you? Ha!

Or you can live your one precious life according to your own light.

Live it loud. And live it in full color.

# Daylilies

In July, daylilies bloom in all their shades of orange. Even though some of them are called pink or purple or even white, an orange hue is hiding in there somewhere.

When I was new to daylilies, I yearned for pink ones, but every so-called pink was more like peach, coral, apricot, or melon. Put a pink daylily next to a truly pink flower, and my eyes cringe. A rose-colored daylily fades to baked salmon.

I bought many varieties of daylilies, and, over time, I gave them away. Being prolific, I then found daylilies springing up where I had dug them out, even where I had laid the bare tubers on the ground for just a few minutes.

We want and we don't want. Sometimes we want and don't want the same thing. As the old adage says, "Be careful what you wish for. You may get it."

I had the stress of yearning for daylilies, the stress of digging them out, and now I have the stress of their reappearance.

I've stopped wishing for flowers, and I've stopped making lists of flowers I want. Flowers show up in my gardens, and some of them are daylilies.

I first had my colors done in 1982. This was before the summer/fall/winter/spring scheme entered our language.

You don't hear much about people having their colors done anymore, maybe because everyone is wearing black or perhaps a daring gray. Beige is also good. You'd think we were a society of Puritans who only had access to white sheep and black sheep or that the only dye we have is onion skins.

Anyway, when I had my colors done, the colorist told me that people have either orange undertones to their skin or blue undertones. I have blue; my sister has orange. She's a fall (and her birthday is in October); I'm a winter (and my birthday is in December.)

Since we had our colors done together by her friend Kay, my sister wears only peach with a dash of spice colors—cinnamon, sage, or saffron.

I keep my distance from orange because it's not even in the palette of colors that people with blue undertones should wear. I don't wear orange, and I don't want orange flowers in my garden.

So after collecting pink or even purple (purple with more orange than red in it) daylilies, I started giving all my daylilies away. All that strappy foliage for a flower that lasts one day? I'll invest in more interesting foliage with longer-lasting blooms. If you like daylilies, I'll be happy to give you mine.

# Partridge Road on Spring Equinox: Nine Houses, Three Seasons, One Road

NINE HOUSEHOLDS SHARE THE two-thirds-mile-long private road I live on, and, at spring equinox, it becomes a three-season road.

The first two-tenths mile has four driveways, the lineup of nine mailboxes, and the dumpster. A lot of cars come and go on this section of Partridge Road, which was named Partridge for the fact that it is part-ridge as well as that partridges reside on the lower section of the road. This part of the ridge faces due south, and the road is smooth, dried-out dirt. The lawns of the four houses here look like spring is coming; the snow has mostly melted off the brown grass.

The next two-tenths miles climb steadily up through a pine forest, gaining fifty feet of elevation. Here, mud season is in full force with ruts deep enough that my car bottoms out every time I travel through. No matter how hard I try to stay out of the ruts and put my tires on the four-inch width of mud that has squished up between other ruts, eventually one rut grabs a tire, the car swerves, and I hang on to the steering wheel for dear life while accelerating as fast as I dare. The snow still covers the forest floor here under the pines, but is tinged brown by the five households of ten cars that travel back and forth here every day.

Then two driveways veer off—one to the right, one to the left, and we enter the winter wonderland of upper Partridge Road. Here, the road is covered with icy white snow that crunches under the tires. Another neighbor turns into his driveway, and now there are only the two houses/four cars at the end of the road silently gliding home to yards where the snow is still a foot deep.

I kid my neighbor Connie, on the lower section, that she lives in the Banana Belt, and sometimes in the spring, when she's not looking, I actually do go down and plant a banana tree from my greenhouse in her flowerbed. The altitude difference between us is fifty feet. On spring equinox, I realize I'm not joking. On one road on one day, three seasons at the same time—spring, mud season, or winter. Name your season.

# Run-Ins

I'M HAVING RUN-INS WITH the material world. Walking into writing group, I tripped over the cat. Earlier, I stumbled over a shoe and then stubbed my toe on the edge of the carpet. I am apparently not watching where I am going.

Yesterday I hip-checked the kitchen table, knocked my knee on the garden cart, and cut the corner too close while rounding into my office.

Being on a collision course with the material world does not sound like a good idea. I'm trying to be extra cautious while driving—sticking to the speed limit and looking both ways at an intersection at least two or three times.

Do I assume that the way will automatically open for my body? That just because it's "me," there will be space?

It is true that I'm not seeing as well as I used to. Yes, my bifocal contact lenses correct my vision to 20/20, but reading labels is hard work. I stopped reading Doonesbury a couple of years ago because I couldn't focus on the thin print in the balloons. Now I mostly skip the entire comics page.

Maybe I should start wearing the necklace that doubles as a glasses holder. Just give up on the idea that I can see, which I often can, as long as all the conditions are right—enough light and big print.

But how about watching where I am going? While

loading the car at the end of a camping trip, I hefted the tent and my forehead right into the hatchback of my Prius. Blood gushed out, but fortunately the first-aid kit was sitting on the ground waiting for embarkation. A band-aid applied to forehead, with blood stains on my left hand and forearm, I returned to loading boxes of leftover food and drinks and a milk crate of camping pots and pans.

Maybe the message is to slow down. Walk, don't jog. When the speed-limit sign says 40 mph on Route 5, take my foot off the accelerator and put the car on cruise control. It's okay to slow-poke my way through my day. Stop rushing—off to the opera this afternoon or into the house.

And for Pete's sake, watch out for the cat.

# My Medicare Card

I received my Medicare card on October 1 and I am thrilled, even though my actual coverage doesn't start until the first day of December. I feel like a high school graduate anticipating college.

The seniors—Bill, for instance—say, "So what? Big deal," but turning 65 is one of those passage years. And my most valuable birthday present is that I won't be paying Blue Cross Blue Shield $533 a month any longer. That's a several thousand dollar "gift" in the first year alone.

As the oldest child in my family (isn't "child" an odd word to use at this age?), I immediately sent an e-mail to my sister and two brothers. Beau utterly enjoys his role as the youngest and takes every opportunity to rib me about being old, so I knew I was letting myself in for it. On the other hand, it's my opportunity to rub his face in the fact that he too is aging. He has a sister old enough to be on Medicare, and that means he has only seven years left until he, too, is "old."

Just two more months until I'm a certified senior. No longer do I have to be confused about which definition to use: 55? 60? 62? I am old. And to celebrate, I'm having a trapeze installed in the attic of my new garage.

Yes, I'm taking Trapeze 101 for the seventh time, and I'm not bored with it. My biceps are firm, even though I still have wings for underarms. I have trapeze calluses on the palms of my hands. But most of all, I'm having fun growing old, teetering on the edge of the aging body and balancing on one foot on the trapeze.

# Buying a Second Home

I AM PART OF A co-housing project in Putney, mostly because I love the idea and want to support it. The prospect of moving into 1,400 square feet? Well, that's something altogether different.

Bill's parlor grand piano is six feet long and five feet wide, but the volume it takes up is much more than thirty square feet or 2 percent of the floor space of this new condo. Bill plays the piano morning, afternoon, and night. While he's playing in the northeast corner of the basement at 10:00 p.m., I'm in bed, reading, ready to fall asleep in the southwest corner of the second floor. In other words, I'm as far away from the piano as I can be.

As a meditator and a writer I require silence. Musician Bill requires music. One of three radios in our house is at his bedside, the other is near the kitchen table, and the third is in his music studio in the basement. If he's not playing classical music, he's listening to it.

While he's eating breakfast and listening to NPR at 9:00 a.m., I'm hiding in my office upstairs, at my computer with the door closed, trying to write Sunday's Dharma talk.

Imagine us smooshed together in half as much space as we have now.

I can't. One of us will have to be dead.

That's another reason I've invested in this independent living community. If I die first, Bill needs people, and of these five other households there are two opera buffs and one alto in the community chorus. Bill-the-extrovert will be much happier living in Putney village than at the end of a dirt road in Dummerston.

Meanwhile, our three-story house at the end of Partridge Road satisfies my need for space and for quiet. I have gardens; Bill has trees; and, together, the two of us have a loving companionship.

# The To-Do List

I'M GIVING UP WRITING to-do lists, but sometimes, my anxiety level is so high that I not only write a to-do list, I make out a schedule of when "to do" what. That's because I'm organizing the Putney Community Dinner this Friday evening. Our Putney Commons group is planning to serve 180 people.

The last time I did this, everything sort of organized itself. One person made the dessert, four people made chili, and I did the salad. Hmmm. Wonder who did the bread?

This year the dessert woman has her third diagnosis of cancer, and is in Thailand on a three-week meditation retreat. One other person in our group of six doesn't like these dinners and, in fact, doesn't particularly like potlucks. So I told her to not prepare anything. She'll show up to serve the dinner.

That leaves four of us to cook.

Two people are making dessert for 30, one is doing the dairy-free, non-gluten entree for 30, and her husband is making the salad dressing. That leaves me to do mac and cheese for 80, pesto for 100, salad and garlic bread for 180, drinks and brownies for 100.

I've asked various other people to help, but friends seem daunted when I ask them to do a salad for 30. Four people will show up to wash dishes. Bill will be one of two waiters, making sure diners have what they need (e.g., water, coffee, dessert) and clearing and re-setting the tables.

Now you can see why I have a to-do list.

I really do enjoy these Second Friday Community Dinners. Various organizations in the town of Putney (population 2,000) volunteer to cook each month—the town government, the Putney Food Co-op, all the writers in Putney, the Putney Historical Society, the Putney School (a private prep school), the Putney Grammar School (a private K–8 school), the Greenwood School (a private school), Putney Central School (the public K–8 school), Putney Cares, the Putney Medical Office, etc. There are enough organizations in town that we at Putney Commons only sponsor this dinner once every three years.

These Community Dinners are a great service to the community. The last time we did this, I noticed a horde of parents with small children arriving promptly at 5:30. Dinners are paid for by donation; some people put nothing into the donation jar; others drop in a $20 bill. It's noisy; it's fun. You see people you haven't seen for a while; you sit next to people you wouldn't ordinarily socialize with.

When I feel daunted by my to-do list, I try to remember my purpose: to be of service by serving dinner. This exercise in catering the dinner is turning out to be a great opportunity to clean out my freezer. What else did I think I was going to do with those stacks of half-pint containers of frozen basil pesto and garlic scape pesto? Bags of frozen grated zucchini make delicious blond brownies. May is a perfect month to clean out the freezer to make room for this summer's harvest.

My schedule begins in earnest on Wednesday, when I make the mac and cheese. Thursday is pesto day and salad prep, which means grating carrots and cabbage and going to pick up the at-cost lettuce at the Putney Coop. Friday is put-it-all-together day.

After that, I'm swearing off macaroni and cheese, I'm swearing off to-do lists, and I may just swear off cooking, too.

I'm going back to the nothing-to-do list.

# Waking Up

I used to fight with my alarm clock. It would ring at 6:45. I'd snooze a few more minutes, maybe fall asleep, and then jolt out of bed at 7:30 to be at work by 8:00.

After a year or so, I decided to stop fighting. I put my little analog alarm clock in a drawer and didn't even look at it.

I began waking up at 6:30, all by myself, happy to start a new day. I had enough time to wander out to the vegetable garden before I left for work, and I arrived at work a few minutes early—my preferred mode—so that I could get a head start on the workday.

My morning mind is clear and raring to go—so much better than the logy mind hazed by an extra hour of stolen sleep. The mind that's already tired from wrestling with itself: *"Time to get up." "No, I don't want to."*

Fifteen or 45 minutes of that argument is enough to wear anyone out.

My father would wake my sister and me up by flicking on the overhead light. "Rise and shine," he'd say. "Smile."

My sister and I would obey. Better not let begrudgingness show, or we'd really be in trouble.

When I got older, I could rebel against my alarm clock. But really, I could say, the rebellion was because I didn't have a reason to get out of bed.

In college, it was easy to get up at six, so I could do calculus for an hour before breakfast. Calculus was not only fun; that hour of the day fit my biorhythms better than the usual college student routine of sleep late, straggle to class, read in the afternoon, and study till midnight. I went to bed at ten.

After calculus, what was there to get up for? It took me a decade to discover gardening.

The gardens still call me out of bed. Or sometimes it's the first chirp of a bird at dawn. The birds need to be fed. That thought gets my bare feet padding down the hallway and down the stairs to the deck where the bird feeder stands empty.

My friend Rebecca believes that her spirit guides call her awake at four in the morning, and sometimes I wonder if this might be true. Like Rebecca, I sometimes wake up, wide awake in the dark, and a paragraph of writing comes to me. Yesterday's problem is suddenly solved, often rather elegantly. Is this "message" a gift from my spirit guides?

The thought—or the smell—of breakfast gets some people out of bed, but I don't feel hungry until nine or ten in the morning.

Oh, how grateful I am to be freed from the schedule of "should" and "supposed to"! How enlivened I feel to get out of bed when I wake up, even when that's four in the morning! I no longer worship sleep, nor long for its soporific effect. Sleep comes when it's good and ready. Wakefulness too.

Some friends complain of broken sleep, as if sleep is supposed to be whole. Sometimes, I sleep for a whole hour, wake up, pee, sleep another whole hour, wake up, pee, and then maybe sleep an actual three hours in a row. And really, that is good enough. I can live on five hours of sleep, even though I prefer six or, in the winter, seven. Resting and deep relaxation count as sleep, even if the mind is still slowly turning the pages of the self it wants to be.

Wake up when you wake up. The clock tells us the time is Now. It says the same thing every time we look at it. Now. Now. Now. Why argue with Life? The body is ready; the body is awake; it's only the mind that has its own opinions. The mind *says* it needs more sleep. But it's awake. Duh.

Wake up, you little sleepy head that is dreaming of more sleep.

Wake up to Life.

# Pen-Challenged

RECENTLY I HAVE BECOME pen-challenged. I don't know why, but I am unable to keep a pen in my new purple pocketbook.

I was sure I had a ten-year supply of pens at home. I picked up two this morning—one had no ink; the other was a pencil. I happened to find the pen I'm writing this with in my vest pocket. That seems like a convenient place, a pen in every pocket—but not, apparently, in my pocketbook.

The drawer under the phone at home used to have five pens in it. Since I seldom sit in the living room, I thinned the pens down to two. One—my favorite paua-shell pen from New Zealand—ran out of ink last week, and I can't figure out how to replace the cartridge, which I had ready for the occasion.

The pen drawer in the kitchen has pens—red ink, green ink, and pink ink, and one old felt-tip that is frayed and widened with age.

My stash of pens is upstairs in my office, and I've been raiding it almost every day. Where do pens go?

Yes, I know I could pick up a year's supply of pens at either of the banks I go to, but I'm loathe to take too much plastic. The forest-green TD Bank pens look nice, but they're not "green," and anyway I prefer the blue ink of the Brattleboro Savings & Loan pens.

I'm sure the banks are happy to have you take as many as you want, assuming you'll inadvertently leave them somewhere when you're writing a check. Then some stranger will find herself writing with a Brattleboro Savings & Loan pen and look at it and think, "Maybe I'll put my money there."

One place I wouldn't put my money is with my pens. I'd never find it.

# Living (and Sleeping) with Restless Legs

Restless Legs Syndrome is called a sleep disorder because it interferes with sleep. One foot or the other (usually not both together, at least for me) contracts into a flexed, pointed, or sickled foot. A slight tickling, crawling sensation runs in a thin line down the entire leg until the foot can't tolerate it and automatically twitches. Or kicks the person sleeping next to you in bed.

Twitching happens about every ten seconds when I'm *relaxed*, but not asleep—for instance, during a massage or an acupuncture appointment. If I don't fall asleep immediately at night, restless legs are very likely to show up. Or if I fall asleep but am then awakened when my bedmate comes to bed an hour later, restless legs will flare up while I'm spooned into him, trying to shade my eyes from his reading light.

I take a calcium-magnesium supplement just before going to bed. Calcium is hard to digest, so why not take it at night instead of in the morning? To tell you the truth, I'm not a good pill-taker, so I'm happy to have fewer supplements to take after breakfast.

Since I am postmenopausal, my nurse practitioner recommends that I take 1,250 mg of calcium. Magnesium has an anti-insomnia effect, but we shouldn't take magnesium alone; it needs to be balanced with calcium. I keep the cal-mag bottle in the medicine cabinet in the upstairs bathroom, right above my toothbrush.

I discovered the importance of *cold feet* on retreat. After the sun goes down, if I get relaxed, the twitching hour arrives. So when I'm at a concert or on an airplane or on retreat, I take off my shoes and yes, even my socks. I sit there barefoot, even in winter.

Having cold feet prevents the arrival of the twitching/restlessness. In bed, I stick my feet outside the covers.

Thank goddess for *homeopathic remedies*. The naturopath started me with Hypericum perfoliatum (a.k.a. Saint John's wort) and Zincum. I dole out four of these tiny sugar tablets and let them dissolve under my tongue. If a single dose of one of them doesn't mitigate the twitching, I take the other.

Zinc can be found naturally in green leafy vegetables and in pumpkin seeds.

Many people walk (or pace) to relieve the creepy-crawly sensations in the feet and legs, but I find that *balancing on one foot* often overrides the restlessness long enough for me to fall asleep. But first I have to wake up enough to (a) get out of bed, and (b) stand on the affected foot without touching anything. I usually stand in a door frame in the dark so I can reach out to find my balance if I start to fall over.

Balancing on one foot for three minutes feels like an eternity when I'm tired. It's important for the foot to do all the work of balancing. If I hold on to the wall or door frame, the foot does not get an entire balancing workout. It doesn't "wake up" sufficiently. So standing on one foot with assistance does not work. Young people can balance on one foot for thirty seconds without even thinking about it; older people lose this natural balancing ability. So I figure that standing on one foot is a great exercise that I will be thankful for when I become decrepit.

Restless legs syndrome often has a *genetic component*. My brother Paul has it, but my sister and youngest brother don't. So sometimes it's just the luck of draw of the gene pool.

And while doing research for this article, I stumbled onto this little factoid: *Sleep with a bar of soap* in your bed. Who know why it works? Who cares? I'll try anything to calm down my legs so that I can just go to sleep.

Restless legs are an uncomfortable combination of torpor and restlessness, but they don't balance each other out. It's odd that the legs become restless and "need" to move just when the body is on the verge of sleep. Tired as it is, the whole body becomes rest-less, unable to fall asleep even while craving sleep. Although the physical pain is negligible, my hatred of this particular bodily affliction and the anguish caused by lack of sleep is a form of torment.

I often project my frustration onto the nearest available object: "Why did you wake me up?" I accuse Bill. "You know that if I'm woken up three times right after I've gone to sleep, I'll have an attack of restless legs and won't be able to go back to sleep for an hour or two."

He strokes my back and is soon snoozing, while I go through my routine of homeopathic remedies and standing on one foot in the dark. Since restless legs result from a neurological dysfunction, and there is no cure, I live with this annoying condition by using remedies that sort of work, sometimes.

Restless legs are the price I pay for living in this particular body. Other people pay other prices for their particular afflictions. The desire, that oh-so-strong midnight desire, *not* to have restless legs is not an option. I can ameliorate the annoying and sometimes tormenting sensations, but in twenty years I haven't been able to erase them. I manage the restlessness as best I can. There are worse things than cuddling up with a bar of soap.

# Lost

We're so busy hanging on to things, we don't notice that we're losing something every second. We say "I lost track of time" as if time were a thing, as if keeping track were possible.

This belief, this illusion, distracts us from the reality of having and losing that happens every second. We want to believe in a continuum—a continuum of time and of a continuous self. But that's not actually true. Take a look and see for yourself.

We lose time, and we lose track of time every second, every moment. We lose awareness that it is always *now*. The body is always here now. The past is only a thought happening now—right now. The future is a thought happening now—right now. Since it is *always* now, since the body can never be anywhere else other than now, how can we lose time? There is no time. There is no time like the present because it's the only time there ever is.

We think today is a continuum that began with waking up, peeing, getting dressed, eating breakfast, drinking a cup of tea, and driving to writing group. All those events are only thoughts that are happening now. We've lost them all already. Gone. Dead. Kaput.

Right now there is only writing, and really not even that. Just a pen scribbling on blue lines of paper. Each word appearing in my mind, each letter written. Then I decipher all those swirls and curlicues and call them words, sentences, paragraphs, stories.

The continuum is a myth. To explain this continuum, we invent a self. Then we lose "our" self and reinvent another one. And so on, throughout the day, until we lose consciousness at night. Even then we are haunted by more dream-thoughts of self. But when we wake up, we know we've been dreaming. That was an experience that I alone had. It was "just a dream," and we shove off that dream-self as unreal. Now we're awake—or so we think. Now we are in a mutually agreed-upon reality of coffee, writing group, morning.

But really, we've lost track of our not-self, the knowing that co-arises with the phenomena of the moment. And we lose every single bit of it all the time. Gone. Dead. Kaput.

We think we've just put that self aside for a moment, and that we'll pick up where we left off. I'll pick up that thought, that train of thought, and then I'll be the same person I was before.

Impossible.

Have you noticed all the things that are lost between one moment and the next? Breath. Heartbeats. Even losing sight of what we're seeing, which seems like a continuum, but we haven't noticed the eye blinks. We believe in the movie of today as if it were not a series of film frames separated by the blink of an eye. "Out there" runs together into a seamless whole, unseen for what it is—just seeing, which arises and is then lost.

We get lost in the mind that is busy stitching it all together. Actually, we've lost our mind, which is simply registering seeing, hearing, and feeling, both in the external world, but more often in the internal world. We hear the internal world and call it thinking. We see the internal world and call it dreaming, imagining, or visualizing. We feel the internal world and call it emotions. This is the activity of the mind that we lose track of.

We stitch all these internal and external worlds together and call it "Mine." Yet "mine" is dissolving every second, like ink flowing onto paper, never the same ink. Always different. Every thought dissolving. Ungraspable. You can't clutch onto it, no matter how hard you try. You lose track all the time. Every word, every sentence, every story forgotten in the next moment.

We're lost, all lost, but there's no need to feel like a lost soul because we're also losing the I-ness of the soul every moment. What do we think is so perpetual about the soul anyway?

We're lost in space. Lost in the spaciousness of here and now where there is only the miracle of knowing.

# Love Changes

Have you noticed how the people you love change? I mean, how your love shifts and changes?

As a child, I loved my mommy and daddy dearly. Then, ten years later, I couldn't get far enough away from them. I traveled to Europe; I moved to Florida, then Utah, then Hawai'i, then Vermont—staying as far away as possible from the Hoosier heartland.

When I was five years old, I loved my sister and brother dearly. I would have laid down my young life for either one of them. Now I seldom call my brother or sister. They seldom come to visit me. My sister hasn't come to see me in 22 years. I go see her once a year in Idaho, and the two of us convene at our brother's house in Indiana every year.

Love is still running underground, although it seems displaced from its original course, when it ran freely and happily overground like the Brandywine Creek near our house.

Nowadays, we're all in love with our little grandchildren. And our sister? Our brother? Well, that love is taken for granted. It's not the juicy young love of a grandchild, who is so glad to see you they call your name while they are still strapped in their car seat, and then they run up and hug your knees. You are smitten. You fall in love with their openheartedness.

Is that what we do? Keep chasing a juicier love? Those old ones, well, we see their faults, their shortcomings, and they see ours.

But to our little children, and then to our sweet, sweet grandchildren, we are sinless. And that's just how we would like to see ourselves.

# Free as a Bird

Am I being true to myself by creating a self? A self that needs to be maintained, a self that can't lark off into new territory, can't owl in the dark night, but stays indoors—mindlessly zoning out? Am I just trying to play it safe because a bird in the hand of grasping is worth two in the tree of life?

The cardinal rule is this: Don't flinch. Don't duck the present moment. Don't worry what others may think. Don't be a chicken about living right up to your edge. Go ahead. Be a nut: hatch new plans. Try out your wings. Jaywalk through life.

What's the use of multitasking and running around like a chicken with its head cut off? Are you on the wild goose chase of family, career, and money, assuming that these things will make you happy? Are you so focused on feathering your nest that you've forgotten how to relax?

Don't be a booby. Don't parrot what others tell you. You won't egret following your bliss. Hawk your truth. Be a silly goose if that's what happens. Old coots can be characters. Go ahead and crow. Warbler your zest for life. Authenticity is as scarce as hens' teeth.

Do you really want to grouse about life? Are you raven mad? Do you really need to flip the bird? Why rail against life? You might be mad as a wet hen, but you are alive!

Let's talk turkey. Take the bird's-eye view. Tern your eyes toward death, and let it be your advisor. Don't gull yourself into thinking you have all the time in the world. One of these days, you'll be dead as a dodo. No one wants to be bittern when they die. Prepare for your swan song.

I want to be veery clear, my little chickadee: We don't have time to sparrow. Crane your neck, stretch it out, let people see your vulnerability. Life itself is your precious nest egg. Don't let your past be the albatross around your neck. The chickens will come home to roost. Keep on puffin. Spread your wings and you can fly like an eagle.

# Great Blue Heron

A GREAT BLUE HERON LANDED near my fishpond in July. It's the moment I've been dreading. I had hoped that my four-foot-wide pond was too small and would escape the notice of a great big heron.

I've heard stories about these kings of fishermen. They can spear every fish in the pond and leave it silently bereft of aquatic life.

I know frogs and salamanders will find this waterhole again. My nephews, ages seven and ten, helped me start digging the hole 24 summers ago. Of course, we didn't get too far the first day because the boys wanted to go catch some frogs. So I drove them to a local pond and watched as they terrorized the frog populace for an hour or so. These were desert boys, unaccustomed to green. Although they lived in the Evergreen State of Washington, they lived in the southeast corner where the dry-land wheat fields roll on for miles. So they loved ponds, frogs, and sticks. They'd walk through the woods, whacking their sticks on every tree.

We returned home to find our hole had become a big mud puddle, and a frog had already taken up residence.

So when the frogs and salamanders disappear, as they may when the pond is locked in by ice in the winter and the water becomes anaerobic, I know that some frogs will smell the water in the spring and find their way there.

But the fish? Those goldfish were born in that pond, and that's another story.

After the great blue heron flapped away, I went to look. The fish were still there, hiding under the lily pads, although I couldn't find the big speckled shubunkins or the white one with the yellow nose. A day or two later, I could finally see they were all still alive.

My slender hope is that the fishpond is too deep for the heron. The pond drops straight down three feet. I've seen herons wading in water up to their ankles and even up to their knees, but I've never seen one standing in hip-deep water.

Standing on the little terrace around the fishpond would require the heron to bend far lower that simply touching his beak to his toes; he'd have to touch his heart to his toes.

Disaster averted, I breathed a sigh of relief.

The next week, a visitor to my flower garden pointed to the sky and said, "Hey, look! There's a great blue heron!"

# Compost Pile:
# A Ten-Minute Writing Exercise

*(In this exercise, the facilitator calls out a word every thirty seconds, which is then incorporated into the writing. The writers have no idea what the next word will be. The word list is in bold print.)*

My **motto** is "**Hidden** in plain view." That's where I like to put my compost piles. *Piles* plural because I **divide** the one I'm adding to from the one that's resting. That way there's no **temptation** to just keep throwing the kitchen scraps on top of only one pile.

Most people feel **ignorant** about composting, but I say, "Make it part of the **landscape**." Let those **blind** worms work silently on the **sticky** garbage that you just **discover**ed at the back of your refrigerator. It's growing blue moldy hair, but the vegetable devas will **forgive** you if you feed the leftovers to the compost pile. Add in a few dead leaves from the **branch** of a tree, and you'll have the right balance of green and brown, creating **medicine** for your gardens. Compost inoculates the soil.

If you feel **swamp**ed with garbage or with deadheading, just throw those dead **ivory** marigolds into the compost.

Compost bins constructed from pallets are very easy to **operate**, and the compost is very **nourish**ing for your gardens. Yes, **animal**s will come to visit, but I don't mind feeding chipmunks, squirrels, and even skunks with that **cream**y white stripe down their back.

Water your compost pile with whatever goopy **liquid**s you have. You can't **destroy** compost. It just keeps on composting; it just decays.

# Best of the Blog 2012
## Impermanence

www.themeditativegardener.blogspot.com

# The Momentary Fragrance of Easter Lilies

My sweetie plays the organ at church, and on Easter Sunday, he brought home an Easter lily. We enjoyed its blooms all week, but the greatest pleasure is walking into the house at night. The deep fragrance of Easter lily hits our nostrils. It smells like heaven.

As we well know, the sense of smell very quickly acclimates, and, after a minute or two, we no longer smell the wonderful scent.

Our other physical senses—taste, touch, seeing, and hearing—also acclimate. We fill up on one taste, and think we are full, but we then mysteriously have room for dessert (a different flavor). People who live near busy streets or airports or railroad tracks don't even hear the noise anymore.

We tune out 95 percent of our experience, so we can pay attention to whatever is changing. Our sixth sense—the mind—stays extremely busy, leading us from one train of thought to another. Our mind is always "changing," and that's where our attention goes. Some of us "live" in our mind.

One definition of mindfulness is "keeping mind together with body." Bring the mind to the body sitting. Right now.

Notice what your hands are doing. Pay attention to your feet. Notice reading and the movement of the eyes.

Notice life.

# Flowerpot Inventory

Because I give away hundreds of plants each year, I have an extensive inventory of used pots. I keep the nice-looking ones, the hanging baskets, and the terra cotta pots in the cellar. The run-of-the-mill plastic pots, I hide behind my compost piles for easy access; my usual routine is

1. pick up a pot
2. plop in a plant
3. fill with compost
4. water.

My sweetie objects to my helter-skelter collection of pots because it looks messy. "But," I say, "you and I are the only ones who see them because they're hidden from public view by the compost bins, which are themselves hidden."

Finally, I stack the whole mess of pots neatly and store them in the woodshed. The impetus? A tree leaning at a sixty-degree angle next to the compost pile is going to be cut down.

I know my flowerpot collection is valuable only to me. If I died tomorrow, they would all be thrown in a dumpster, or better yet, taken back to the recycling program where I got them in the first place.

All our collections are slated for dispersal—our knick-knacks, our housewares, our furniture. Even our collection of friends shifts and changes slightly from year to year as people move away, or we ourselves move or change jobs.

Everything I cherish will change and vanish. Even my collection of flowerpots.

# Goodbye, Dear Hemlock

For years, I've been parking my car under a hemlock tree. I call it my "hemlock garage" because its evergreen branches keep the snow off my car in the winter and the sun off my car in the summer.

In April, a logger is coming to cut down the hemlock (and ten other trees), in preparation for building an actual garage.

Goodbye, dear hemlock.

Change is difficult, even when we bring it upon ourselves. We want, *and* we don't want. On the horns of this dilemma, the mind fights a civil war with itself, and peace is nowhere to be found.

Change is happening every minute, every second. When we recognize this truth, we begin to break through the illusion that we call "reality." We begin to break out of the dream state we normally walk around in.

I'm going outdoors now to wrap my arms around my dear hemlock tree.

## Clearing

Impermanence has struck again. The logger cut down six trees yesterday, and my side "yard," which was really only an herb garden, is now quite spacious and airy.

Sometimes, it's time to clear away portions of our life—relinquish a toxic relationship, turn loose of some responsibilities or a volunteer job, renounce an addictive habit, opt out of e-mail newsletters.

Even though letting go is difficult, we are rewarded with a feeling of "Ahhh." Now we can breathe again. Now we can see the forest for the trees.

In my side yard, some trees have been sacrificed. Now I can see more clearly.

## Spring Springs Up

Fiddlehead ferns are unfurling. It's time to eat spring.

In the herb garden, the French sorrel is ready to leap into a lemony soup, and the Egyptian (or walking) onions somersault into salads, stir-fry skillets, and sauces of all sorts.

The lawn grows violets and dandelion greens in profusion—perfect for a spring-tonic salad.

In pockets of lime-rich soil in the woods, wild leeks grow in abundance.

Change is happening at a rapid rate as spring springs up all around us. Let's eat spring and thereby be ourselves changed.

# My Herb Garden Changes—and Vanishes

A local garden club tours my spring garden in early May. Does my garden look good? Of course. It's spring! I have lots of spring-blooming flowers—*Leucojum* (summer snowflake), *Lunaria* (money plant), and *Phlox divercata* (woodland phlox) accent the spaces between the narcissus and jonquils.

Do I feel ready for the garden tour? Of course not. My herb garden is half torn apart due to excavation, which will start the next day.

Everything I cherish will change and vanish. My dear herb garden is changing and vanishing. Next month, two trenches will be dug through it to connect utilities from the house to the little guest room attached to the garage. Tomorrow, four feet of dirt will be piled on top of the back half of the herb garden. It will be a mess out there. Now, it's just a pre-mess.

*Everything* I cherish will change and vanish, including myself. These "little" changes are just preparing me for the big event.

# Dead Phlox

I was a naughty girl.

I bought a purple phlox in mid-August, but didn't plant it. When I came home from a retreat a week later, it was still standing on the front step, but now it had withered brown leaves and dried-up flowers.

Of course, I hoped it wasn't really dead yet. I hoped some end-of-life artificial hydration would resuscitate it, so I soaked it with water.

This disappointment is the result of desire. I saw the purple phlox in a friend's garden; I stopped at the greenhouse on the way home and bought it. Then doubt and procrastination intervened. I had the object of my desire in hand, but I couldn't ramp up the desire to take the next step and plant it. I couldn't decide where to put it. I didn't want to clear a spot for it. It languished for a week, looking sadder and sadder. Then I left home for a week.

We want things to stay like we leave them: we want permanence. But unwatered plants change—they wither and die while we're not looking. When we look again, life has changed. The life of the purple-phlox-in-a-pot changed to death.

The ego can load more suffering onto itself (*It's all my fault!*), because that way we at least have a reason for what happened. We load more stress on top of the disappointment over and over again. Really, all that happened was that a plant died. Life dies. Sooner or later. This phlox died sooner than I wanted it to.

Life is not permanent.

## Harvesting before Frost

The race is on to see how much I can harvest before frost. September morning temperatures hover around forty degrees.

There's not too much left in the garden, and that's good, because there's not too much space left in the freezer.

The tomatoes are in, leaving just a basketful of cherry tomatoes on the vine. The winter squash are in, but one gourd vine went crazy. I try to bring in one gourd every time I return from the garden. Then there are my eight varieties of basil.

We plant many seeds during our lifetime—friends, family, career, spiritual path, service to others. Which shall we harvest? And which do we just let go of?

Many friends come and go. Our career ends. *Family* changes definition: our parents die, our siblings drift into the distance, wives and husbands divorce, our children grow up, our grandchildren live far away. Who *is* our true family?

Our spiritual path may ebb and flow, yet it gives us the ability to harvest kindness, mindfulness, and equanimity, no matter the season.

# The End of Summer Vacation

The houseplants came indoors at the end of September after a good long summer recess of more than five months.

The *Dieffenbachia* looks great. The banana tree is nearly six feet tall.

I had to make some hard decisions. There's just not enough room in my jam-packed solarium for the four-foot-tall jade plant. I'm sending it off to the Plant Sale on Saturday. But first, I sawed off a side shoot, which was 18 inches tall; I'm keeping that little(r) plant.

The bird-of-paradise, which blooms when it is pot-bound, busted out of its pot this summer. I divided it into four pots, one of which I'll keep.

Change. Change of season. Change of plants. Change of plans—the repotting took longer than expected.

All around us, life is in a constant flux of change. Although you don't notice it, you too are constantly changing, even right now while you are reading this page. You've already changed your clothes and changed your mind about something (maybe about the clothes you're wearing.) Breath has changed; blood has changed; bodily fluids have changed—some have been eliminated, some have been added. I'm drinking tea as I write this.

Summer vacation is well and truly over. Someday the summer of our life will drift away.

Welcome fall.

## Storing Life Away

We had our first fire in the woodstove late one September morning, just to take the chill off. Even though it's not really cold yet, it's time for long sleeves and long pants. I'm storing summer clothes away bit by bit—shorts, short-sleeved shirts, tank tops, Capri pants.

Out in the vegetable garden, I'm trying to store summer away. Recently, I made lemon basil pesto and stored it in the freezer.

We try to store our lives away—in photo albums, on Facebook, in memory, on flash drives. These give us the illusion of a continuum. We think we can just reach back and touch our past. Yet our lives actually unfold moment by moment.

That person in the picture that you take to be you is actually nonexistent. We could say she's "dead." The photo reminds us of how we used to look—when we were five or eighteen or thirty, or even yesterday. But there is no way we can reach out and touch that person. She is gone, gone, gone.

Now there is only *this* person, with a memory that is unraveling in the present moment.

# Re-Contoured

The six-foot trench has been filled in. The excavator has moved the dirt, but the contours of the garden and yard have been changed. The flower bed, the strip of lawn, and the edging of shrubs just don't look like they used to.

It's another form of impermanence, sort of like someone who's had a major operation. Afterward, at first, they feel worse, and maybe their loved ones feel they are just a little bit different somehow. Perhaps the anesthesia has induced a shred of mental confusion. How *did* things used to be?

Life and the garden shifts slowly, sometimes subtly, over time, as they organically evolve. But this re-contouring is a big change from one day to the next. And it's not the way I want it; it's the way it actually happened.

The garden's other lesson in impermanence, the stress of wanting things to be different than they are, and the emptiness of the word *garden*, which meant one thing yesterday and a different thing today.

## Baby Green Grass

Remember that six-foot-deep trench that was dug through my white garden in late October? Just beyond that garden the reseeded swath of lawn is sprouting a peach fuzz of fine green grass. The baby grass loved the warmish weather that lasted through November. And now that it's December, I have to trust that the tiny grass will be warm enough this winter with its thin blanket of straw.

It's really quite amazing to watch impermanence in action. Lawn became a six-foot-deep trench became squishy mud became reseeded with a layer of straw became fine green grass. Change happened dramatically and visually.

Our bodies, our senses, our feelings, and our minds change even faster, from second to second. Yet, last evening, when I had dinner with friends from Burma whom I had not seen in five years, the first thing we did was say, "You look the same. You haven't changed at all." But many changes *have* happened: a husband has died, a grandchild has been born.

Fine baby green grass grows on the grave of a loved one.

# Cheryl's Memories

# Mackinac

I WENT TO SCHOOL ON the first day of sixth grade with a handkerchief in my dress pocket because hay fever was clogging my sinuses. By the next day, sneezing, coughing, and wheezing had overpowered my respiratory system, and asthma kept me in bed for a week. One morning I was actually able to walk to the breakfast table, and I sat on the edge of my kitchen chair, using my hands to hold myself up, as if that would give me an extra few millimeters of breathing space. I needed all the breath I could get.

I fully expected my Christian Science father's verdict to be, "You're going to school today." Instead he said, "Get packed. We're driving to Michigan."

I couldn't believe my ears. My fourth-grade sister and first-grade brother walked out the front door and down the driveway to the school bus, and I did not go with them. My three-year-old brother stayed home with Mom, and I got into the front seat of our 1957 two-tone Chevrolet—robin's-egg blue and white. I was four-foot-eight, and I weighed 48 pounds.

Our cars never had radios, and Dad would say, "Let's sing." So we sang "Home on the Range" and "She'll Be Coming around the Mountain" and whatever else I could think of. I played license-plate games as he drove north on two-lane roads, hour after hour. I tried to find words on billboards that began with each letter in alphabetical order.

We each counted animals on our side of the road, but if you passed a cemetery you had to start over. First one to 100 won.

Somewhere in central Michigan, Dad started pulling over at motels and asking if they had foam rubber pillows. Mom had just converted all our feather pillows to foam rubber the previous year because my brother Paul and I were allergic to chicken feathers. Most motels still had feather pillows, but finally on the third or fourth try, we stopped for the night.

The next day we arrived at Mackinaw City, Michigan, and Dad chose a motel of little cabins right at the foot of the brand-new Mackinac suspension bridge.

We soon had a routine of going to nearby Teysen's Cafeteria for breakfast and for dinner. After dinner, we'd drive to the shore of Lake Michigan with stolen packages of oyster crackers, and I'd feed the seagulls.

During the day, Dad drove to Indian burial sites and to Sault Sainte Marie, where we watched iron-ore boats go through the locks between Lake Superior and Lake Huron. We crossed the border into Canada—my first foreign country—but I didn't like it because the pavement was so rough. We took the ferry to Mackinaw Island and rode a horse-drawn carriage around the island.

Then one day Dad drove to the airport in Cheboygan. I saw Mom get off the plane, and Dad got on and flew away.

Mom wasn't as much fun as Dad. She stayed in the car while I fed the seagulls because she didn't want the seagulls to poop on her hair. But things were more orderly, too. With Mom in the cabin, I took my first bath in a week and wore a flannel nightie to bed with her. When I slept with

Dad, I had worn blue jeans day and night. Mom took me shopping and bought me a pair of beautiful gray gabardine trousers. She usually made all my clothes, so having real slacks felt wonderful.

I sent postcards home using the new four-cent stamps that had the Mackinac Bridge on it. I bought souvenirs for my sister and brothers and for my sixth grade class.

Then it was time to drive home. The pollen count in Indiana was low enough, and I had recovered sufficiently that my allergies had calmed down.

I loved Michigan because it felt so cool and clear, and because I could breathe there.

Perhaps what I loved was being on vacation with my dad, a thing that wouldn't happen again for another thirty years. Perhaps I loved being my mother's only child for a few days. Twenty years would pass before she and I took another road trip together. Perhaps what I loved was seeing the world beyond my narrow Hoosier confines. Perhaps I loved that my mother and my dad weren't fighting.

## Things I Believed Were True When I Was a Child

- Daddy is right.
- I love Mommy and Daddy.
- I should be quiet.
- Girls shouldn't talk to boys.
- I shouldn't talk to boys.
- Boys shouldn't talk to me.
- Shooting the breeze is bad.
- It's important to "do."
- Being busy is good.
- I like reading, but I've read all the books in the house, so I have to buy my own books.
- Dad doesn't like me to read so much.
- Dad is proud of the fact that I'm always on the Honor Roll.
- I'm too big. (Therefore I should be small.)
- I should take up very little space.
- I'll get spanked if I do something wrong.
- Mom's spankings don't hurt; she's not really serious. It's funny when she gets mad.
- It's scary when Dad gets mad.

- Be very, very quiet when Dad is taking a nap.
- Don't wake Dad up.
- I'm a nonconformist.
- Girls should be president, too.
- Don't talk on the phone for very long.
- People on the party line listen in so that they can hear what you say on the phone. (There are eight families on the party line.)
- Don't make long-distance phone calls to my girlfriends because long-distance is expensive.
- Dad decides what TV programs we watch after dinner.
- I'm smart.
- Being smart is easy.
- Jesus died for our sins.
- It's a sin to lie or steal.
- I don't want to be a sinner.
- Mom wants to go to church even though she doesn't go very often.
- I don't need to talk to adults.
- Men have more interesting conversations than women.
- Women talk about boring things like recipes.
- Men don't do housework. So my brothers never have to do the dishes or vacuum or dust.
- Girls do dishes. My sister and I take turns doing the dishes every night. (We started doing the dishes when we were six.)

# Recipes from Ten-Year-Old Cheryl

**Crackers in milk**

Crush enough saltines to fill a glass.
Then pour milk over them to the brim of the glass.
Eat with a long-handled iced-tea spoon.

**Open-face mayonnaise sandwiches**

Spread Miracle Whip on a slice of Wonder bread.
(In 1956, I had never heard the word "open-face," and
 I'd never tasted real mayonnaise.)

**Iced Graham crackers**

Put a heaping teaspoon of grape jelly in a cup.
Beat in powdered sugar until the mixture turns to a
 lavender-pink icing.
Spread on graham crackers.

### Wonder Bread sandwiches

Take a slice of Wonder Bread and fold in half.
Fold in half again.
Fold in half again.
And fold in half again.
Smoosh it on the counter with the heel of your right hand.
When Mother says, "That's just a dough ball," you smile while you are chewing.

### Butter and sugar sandwiches

Slather room-temperature butter onto a slice of Wonder Bread.
Sprinkle with white sugar.
Fold in half and eat.

### Cinnamon sugar pie

When Mom makes a pie, I put the leftover crust dough on a cookie sheet, sprinkle with cinnamon sugar, and bake alongside the pie.

### Butter and sorghum on hot biscuits for breakfast

Put a tablespoon of room-temperature butter on the side of your plate.
Add a tablespoon of sorghum molasses.
Whip the butter and sorghum together with your knife into a creamy consistency.
Slather onto a hot biscuit.

### Watermelon with salt

Dad brings home a whole watermelon. Always room temperature.

He takes it out to the picnic table in the backyard. He cuts it in half, and then he slices off a round.

Then he cuts that round into quarters.

Pick up a triangle of watermelon.

Use the big metal popcorn-salt shaker to salt the watermelon.

Throw the rinds over the backyard fence into the woods so Uncle George's white-faced Herefords will eat them.

### Muskmelon with salt and pepper

We never had cantaloupes, only muskmelons at room temperature.

Take a slice.

Salt and pepper it.

Eat it like watermelon. (That is, never use a spoon or fork.)

### Fresh tomatoes

Take the salt shaker into the garden.

Pick a ripe tomato.

Lick a spot so the salt sticks.

**Aunt Jenny's grilled cheese sandwiches**

Use two slices of Wonder Bread.
Cover each slice with Miracle Whip, then with slices of Velveeta.
Put together.
Use room-temperature butter to butter the outsides of the sandwich.
Heat up a cast-iron skillet, and toast the sandwich until the cheese melts.
(Putting on a lid for the last minute speeds up the melting.)


**Raw hot dogs**

Stick close to Dad, who opens the refrigerator and pulls raw hot dogs out of the package.
You get one, too.


**Chocolate milk**

Put three teaspoons of Nestlé's Quik in a glass, even though the box only calls for two teaspoons.
Add milk.
Use your spoon and have fun watching the dry, brown powder bubble up to the top and float on the milk for a few seconds before dissolving.

**Baked bean sandwiches on Sunday night, because Mom didn't cook on Sunday nights.**

Butter a slice of Wonder bread and spread with cold baked beans from the refrigerator, left over from Sunday dinner.

Fold in half.

(Now I call it a "Hoosier taco.")

**Ice cream soup**

On Sunday evenings, we could open the freezer and take out the gallon of A&P vanilla ice cream.

Pour a tablespoon of Nestlé's Quik over it, and mush together with a spoon until it becomes a smooth, cold chocolate "soup."

**Ice cream**

Go outdoors and gather a mixing bowl full of snow.

Add just a little milk and vanilla and enough sugar to make it taste good.

# Wild Strawberries

The June before I left for college, I walked with my ten-year-old brother, Beau-Beau, to the railroad tracks about a quarter of a mile away from our home. Freight trains came through a few times a day to pick up grain at the elevators dotted every four or five miles along its route.

Strawberry season was so short—just a couple of weeks each year—but that day that we went to pick wild strawberries, we had all the time in the world to pick the pinky-fingernail sized bursts of flavor.

"Oh, these are so sweet," Beau-Beau said, and we ate one or two for every one we put into our baskets.

Eventually, on that lazy summer day, we had picked enough.

Back home, we stemmed them until they stained our thumbnails red. Mother baked a batch of biscuits so we could have strawberry shortcake for dessert. Hot biscuits out of the oven split open so that butter melted on the halves while a broad serving spoon ladled the strawberries in their red juice onto the flaky buttered biscuits. Dad shook the can of whipped cream and dispensed a white swirl on top of the tiny berries.

"Oh, these are so sweet," we said.

The next day Mother made wild strawberry jam.

I went off to college, but Beau-Beau ate strawberry jam on biscuits every morning until it was gone.

## Nonnie's Fingers

Even though Nonnie's hands were crippled with arthritis, she kept her fingernails painted a raspberry or cherry red. She who had knit sweaters and slippers for each of her ten grandchildren was finally ready to give it up. But three of us begged her to continue knitting slippers, and so she did.

My sister and I rewarded her by making sure the first present we opened on Christmas morning was the soft package: new slippers, which we called "footies." We immediately put the new footies on our feet, finally discarding last year's slippers, which had great holes in the balls of the feet and the heels. Now a new slippered year could begin.

Nonnie, who taught us knitting, crocheting, tatting, and embroidery, slowed down on all these handicrafts. No more tatted lacy edging for pillowcases or hankies. No more big crocheted afghans. In her eighties, she used up the ends of all those skeins of Red Heart worsted and knit two- or three-inch squares, which she eventually stitched together as a lap robe-sized afghan that looked rather like my first-grade crayon coloring.

In the afternoons of first grade, ancient Mrs. Akers handed out blank pieces of manila paper with a grid of one-inch squares on one side. Some kids drew pictures on the blank side, but I colored each square a different color from my box of twenty-four crayons. That's what Nonnie's final afghans looked like.

When she finally escaped her arthritic, bursitis-ridden body at age 84, I couldn't help but touch those beautiful fingers with the red fingernail polish in the casket. Oh! They were cold. So cold. My dear Nonnie's fingers.

Those fingers had painted ceramics, beginning when she was nearly fifty. While I rolled clay snakes to make a coiled basket, she glazed tiny blue forget-me-nots illuminated by a dash of gold edging. She rolled tiny clay leaves and stuck them together just so, making rosebuds and roses. All to decorate my plain white ceramic basket.

She painted eyelashes on Easter bunny mugs and gave a bare touch of gold to a pink Santa's team of ceramic white reindeer that had pink rhinestone eyes. Open ceramic Bibles with a single verse, Christmas decorations for each of her ten grandchildren. So much glazing, so many glazes and not a single grandchild who was interested in her legacy of molds, glazes, or a kiln.

Instead, we divvied up the shelves and shelves of ceramics, Nonnie's "ceramic gallery," you could say. Some of these dust catchers decorate my home now, reminding me, every time I notice one of them, of my dear, dear Nonnie.

# May 1, 2011

MAY 1, 2011, WOULD have been Nonnie's 108th birthday, and let me tell you, she had some sort of bang-up celebration. That old Taurus liked her stability and security, so she was spreading it around.

As it happened, my sister and I convened in Indiana that weekend for our annual meeting with our brothers. Beau was a bit iffy about us staying at his house because he was trying to sell it. He'd put it on the market the previous summer, and only three people had come to look at it. So he had taken it off the market in November, spent $35,000 making all the changes the realtor told him to make, and put it back on the market in late April.

The weekend we were there, two families came to see the house. One young couple brought all four of their parents and stayed two hours beyond the one-hour viewing. They bought the house a few days later.

My sister, Dona Christine, who carries Nonnie's name—Christine—had had her 8,000-square-foot house on the market for three years. She and her husband were yearning to move closer to their grandchildren in Idaho. Potential sales had fallen through three times. After the first failure, she learned not to move all her furniture out of the house until she had the cash in hand.

That weekend of May 1, Dona and her husband were

just figuring out a deal with the high-plains dry-land wheat farmer from whom they had bought the land in the first place.

Also that weekend, Dona's 33-year-old son, Chris, called in distress. His recent ex-girlfriend was now dating a guy who, four years earlier in a bar, had knocked six-foot-two, 250-pound Chris to his knees and bashed his face into the concrete, then broken the ribs of a young woman. Chris had advised the ex-girlfriend to get rid of this potentially violent guy, and now Chris was afraid for his life. Just sixteen months earlier, his neighbor had been shot and killed at 8:30 in the morning by her irate ex-husband. Chris wanted out of his house and out of town fast.

So Chris fled to his younger brother Calvin in Idaho, who, that first weekend in May was closing his business, Sandpoint Outfitters—a hunting and fishing store. A box store selling hunting and fishing gear was just moving in a few blocks away, so Calvin was going to work for them as an assistant manager.

On Saturday, Dona and I drove up to Lafayette to visit two of Beau's children, both recently graduated from Purdue—Leah with a nursing degree, and Gabe with a master's in mechanical engineering. As we sat around Leah's living room, Gabe and his wife arrived, and I asked her what was cooking.

"I'm ready for a baby," she said, glancing at Gabe.

Lo and behold, nine months later, a baby girl was born on the very day that Nonnie gave birth to her second daughter—January 20. (In the interim, Gabe and his wife did buy a new house, too.)

So, Happy 108th Birthday, Nonnie! You died 23-1/2 years ago, and your grandchildren are thinking of you. But your great-grandchildren barely knew you. They think the sales of their houses and all their moving is happening of its own volition. But I am sure that nothing gives you greater pleasure than to see the people you love happily settled.

# A Narrow Life

I FLEW TO INDIANA IN September 2010 for my 45th high school reunion. From the airport I drove straight to Brownsburg on the west side of Indianapolis, the opposite side from where I grew up. Brownsburg is the county seat of Hendricks County. I grew up in Hancock County on the east side of Indianapolis, whose county seat is Greenfield.

I drove to Brownsburg because I wanted to visit our class valedictorian, Susie Wheeler. I knew she wouldn't attend our class reunion, but I wanted to see her. I had missed her at our fortieth, so I went out of my way, but not really that far out of my way, to visit her.

Susie and I weren't good friends in junior high and high school, but we often sat next to each other—Wheeler, Wilfong—and chatted in the two or three minutes before English or Algebra started. It was clear, even in seventh grade, that Susie would be our class valedictorian. She took books home every evening and studied, assisted by her stay-at-home father, who had been blinded in his first battle during World War II. Susie adored her father.

In fifth grade I had asked my dad to help me with fractions. He yelled at me for ten minutes, and I never again asked him for help with my homework. As a junior I did ask him to buy me a slide rule for chemistry class, and he brought home a really expensive $25 slide rule in a leather case—a Keuffel-Esser slide rule with twenty-eight scales on it. The boys in my class just had flimsy $5 slide rules with eight scales.

My father had no idea how to use a slide rule. He must have asked the engineer who designed his subdivisions what to buy. That slide rule lasted me all the way through Thermodynamics I and II, Strength of Materials, and Quantum Mechanics at Purdue University, where I studied engineering. I finally gave up the slide rule and majored in math because that was easiest.

Susie Wheeler and I went to regional algebra contests together. As freshmen, we placed fifth and sixth. As juniors, I placed fifth and she placed seventh. That was probably the only time I ever bested her. As seniors, she went to Girls' State; I went to the Governor's Youth Council and the Model Legislature.

As we sat in her living room in Brownsburg, she said to her 31-year-old daughter, who lives with her, "Cheryl and I had an unusual relationship because it was so noncompetitive."

I knew from the beginning that Susie would be number one, and I would be number two. She worked for it. I didn't. She deserved it.

Our valedictorian and class secretary went to Ball State Teachers College, married her high school sweetheart, and had two daughters. The year that I was researching my *Following the Nez Perce Trail* book and driving 25,000 miles alone in the wilds of Montana and Idaho, Susie divorced and became a school librarian. The school librarian career seems perfect because she had been a student librarian during our junior and senior years. She loves to read mysteries.

The mystery to me is what happened to Susie's leadership and scholarship. She didn't want to go to the class reunion because she didn't like the way it was organized. As the senior class secretary, she could have elected to organize it herself.

The way my father taught us to swim was the way his father taught him: throw the kid into the creek. He also used the sink-or-swim style for child-rearing. As children, we four were essentially on our own within the narrow confines of our ranch house in the woods. My father's tantrums—while he taught me fractions, for instance—gave me, a reticent child, emotional resilience. A storm would blow through, to be followed by sunny skies within a minute or two.

Susie Wheeler was protected by her adoring father and her hard-working mother, who dressed her in Villager matching sweater and tight-skirt sets. Perhaps when life's inevitable bumps and bruises came along, Susie lost her confidence. Nowadays she stays close to home, preferring to go out to dinner with her married daughter and in-laws rather than come to our class reunion.

And I dare to travel, alone if need be, so that once in a while I can visit people I have loved—like Susie Wheeler.

# My 45th High School Reunion

I set up a Facebook page for my high school class and began connecting with my classmates about three months before our 45th reunion.

I nearly dreaded going to that reunion, because I fully believed I would be the only heathen in attendance, the only person who didn't press Like because Jesus was my savior, and the only person who did not support the Tea Party.

I come from the Midwest—the middle of America—a thousand miles from one coast and 2,000 miles from the other. I have become what my redneck relatives despise—an elite intellectual.

My father thought college graduates, including his own youngest brother, were educated idiots. That opinion hasn't changed in the county I grew up in, where 9 percent of adults have graduated from college and twice that number have dropped out of high school. Rednecks do not appreciate being thought of as stupid, even if they did not graduate from high school. They definitely know how to make intellectuals look stupid, even though, earlier in this paragraph, I tried to make *them* look stupid by saying that high school dropouts far outnumber college graduates.

I brought my new book, *The Meditative Gardener*, to the reunion as a show-and-tell. People politely looked at the cover, but didn't touch it—probably that word "meditative" on the cover. The work of the devil, no doubt. Good thing they didn't see the idolatry of the back cover where there's a picture of a statue of the Buddha.

I continue to be fascinated by people who act like they haven't just heard me say, "Here's my new book that was published last year." That's my line of monologue. Their line is about their family. I listened to long sagas of medical troubles. I heard biting comments, such as: Rachel didn't come because Myrtle said something mean to her last time. "Last time" was five years ago. And that was forty-plus years after their various fallings-out at Wilkinson High School. Aren't we old enough to let this stuff go?

Everyone I know in Indiana goes to church on Sunday morning. Then they spend the rest of the week being mad at their friends or elderly parents or their cousins or at classmates they haven't seen in a coon's age.

The valedictorian, who was also our senior class secretary, refuses to come to reunions because we consolidated schools in our senior year. She doesn't want to talk to or visit with those people from "the other school," and they're the ones who are doing all the organizing of the reunions.

Logic might ask the class secretary why she doesn't organize the students from Wilkinson, but logic seems to have been left behind back when she and I went to the regional algebra contest in 1963.

So I sit at a table of eight Wilkinson people politely talking with people they never talked to in high school, while the fifteen Charlottesville people are finishing off three bottles of wine and laughing so hard they're peeing their pants.

I sit across the table from Dolly Wilson, who sat behind me in third grade looking unkempt, pathetic, and dumb.

Now she's attractive and talkative. She went to beautician school after we graduated. Now she's a housekeeper at the assisted-living facility in Greenfield. She cleans the apartment of Mrs. Cook, our fourth grade teacher, now 95 years old, and Mrs. Orahood, the principal's wife who taught us English and phys ed in junior high.

"I hated school," Dolly says. "Reading didn't click in until fourth grade." Now she's a voracious reader of anything that comes her way, including the abstracts on the piece of land she recently bought, which showed that the land once belonged to Richard Hanna's great-grandmother. Richard sits at the end of the table, scrubbed clean of the dust and chaff he's been stirring up on his 500 acres since dawn. The two-month drought means the corn is ready to pick a month early. All day long as I've driven from visiting one cousin to another to my only remaining aunt to the graveyards of my parents, I've seen a dozen corn pickers racing across fields, stirring up clouds of dust, screeching to a halt at the end of the rows, turning quickly, and racing off in the opposite direction. Richard was a Future Farmer of America 45 years ago, and now he's farming the future—corn for syrup, for soda pop, for ethanol.

Barbara Knox sits next to Dolly. Of the 43 girls in our class, she's the only other woman, besides me, who retains her maiden name. That's because she never married, continues to live in the house she grew up in, and just retired from teaching fourth grade at the school we graduated from. When she and I were in fourth grade, she had her full height and weighed 150 pounds. I was four-foot-six and weighed 45 pounds. Today, I'm taller than she is with her severe dowager's hump.

Next to Barbara sits Linda Trees, whose Church of the Nazarene parents forbade her to wear slacks or gym shorts in P.E., forbade her to dance or play cards. She leaves shortly after looking at my book, as if she's been contaminated.

Louis Calvert and Bob Cottrell worked on the line in nearby rust belt factories until the factories moved to Mexico. Louis was a consultant to a plant in Mexico, located on Avenida NAFTA for six months, and then he "retired" at age 55.

That leaves Margi sitting next to me. My group of friends adopted her when she moved to our school in our junior year, but I never really bonded with her. The year after we graduated she married Marvin, also from our class, and they have four children and a successful denture business. She sings in the choir at their church, which has 1,500 members. She talks and talks and talks, providing the glue our table of familiars needs. Familiar, as we all are to each other, having spent six or twelve years with each other, yet today we are all strangers too.

Even though we have so little in common, we look at each other and travel back in time. I see their seventh-grade, third-grade, first-grade selves, and they remember mine. This is a rare intimacy, reminding us of a time before we thought we were separated by religious and political beliefs, when we simply knew each other.

Endings

# Don't Panic

"Don't Panic" is the motto of *The Hitchhiker's Guide to the Galaxy*. Really, whether you're under the influence of the Improbability Drive—as Arthur Dent and Ford Prefect are for the entire five books of the trilogy (Don't ask, and for god's sake, don't panic, thinking you've just missed something)—or if you are living a mostly harmless life, then panic really is quite useless.

Panic freezes the brain and shuts down creativity. If you're in a possibly panicky situation, just relax. What's the worst that can happen? Death? Death has already been happening every minute, every second of your life. You just haven't noticed.

Where is your four-year-old self? Dead. Where is the one who ate lunch today? Dead. All those photos that you think are pictures of yourself are actually photos of dead people. You don't look like that now, and you never will again. Your whole life is already dead and gone. You just haven't been paying attention.

The Buddha says, "I have long been tricked, cheated, and defrauded by this mind." Our minds trick, cheat, and defraud us, too. We are blind to what is actually going on in the world around us because we are so busy believing every word the mind says. Meanwhile, we are not seeing what's what or what *leads to* what.

Don't panic. We are hitchhiking our way from moment to moment, zooming through the galaxy without even noticing that every thought is gone like a shooting star in space. Energy moves. That's all.

Relax and enjoy the show at the end of the universe.

## Body Trill

Not unusually while on a retreat, as my mind quieted my unfinished business came to haunt me. One day, my particular demon, a woman whom I don't like and don't trust, haunted me all day long. While doing lying-down meditation on my bed one late afternoon, my demon pestered me and pestered me some more. Finally, I silently screamed into my pillow, "I want the truth."

The Void appeared before me. Oh. That was way more Truth than I was asking for, and I had no idea what to do with it. Or how to respond. Of course, there was nothing to do. Perhaps I could have just seen it as a mirror, one that I could look into and see my true nature of emptiness and no-thing-ness. Or, as Krishnamurti says, "Truth is a pathless land." Yep. The Void is pathless, all right.

The thought that I am a solid and separate being is pure illusion. I have seen, on another month-long retreat, that the body is not different from space. Everything I think that I have or that defines me is built in the mind. But I'd rather distract myself with an I/me/mine so that I don't have to look directly into The Void. I'd rather avoid The Void.

\* \* \*

One night during my month-long retreat I woke up with my body vibrating at a high pitch. I wasn't physically moving or vibrating, but my inner experience was as if a wire running from my third toe up my legs, through my vagina and heart, up the back of my neck, and up to the crown of my head was vibrating at a fast trill. My background tinnitus was screaming loudly.

Suddenly I was catapulted into outer space, and I thought, *I am going to die.* I shattered into shards of light.

From a long, long, long way away, I could feel a pulse regularly beating. I could feel breath breathing itself. That had nothing to do with me, and I felt very calm as the loud trilling continued.

Is this what happens when a person meets sudden death? Startling and extremely loud, but very calm as consciousness is hurled back to The Source from which it came, to be dissolved in infinite space so that not a single particle of "I" or "me" remains. Soul loses the respiration of spirit and becomes nameless and formless—unborn and undying.

One of my contemplations on retreat was "*I* and *mine* are two." This means I can be separated from all that is mine—house, car, possessions, my beloved Bill, my sister, my brother, my mind, my memory, my body, even my name, and the thousand other things I call mine.

Gone. Really gone into nothing. No-thing. *Nothing*.

# What Do the Dying See?

One Friday afternoon in August, I went to sit vigil with a sixty-year-old hospice patient named Beth. When I arrived at one o'clock, her oldest son left to go sort things out with his two siblings, and there I was. Alone in a room at the nursing home with a woman I did not know.

Beth had Huntington's disease, formerly called Huntington's chorea, a neurodegenerative disease that causes writhing in its victims. She had elected not to receive artificial hydration or nutrition.

This was the only fact I knew about this woman and I admired her for it. I have made the same decision regarding my durable power of attorney for health care. Several years ago, I went to a workshop with Judy Kinley, a former nurse and now a minister. She said, "Liquids in means liquids out." IVs in means catheter out. Then there are the various infections that can happen.

No, it's better not even to start down that road of tubes running into and, therefore, out of the body.

So there I sat, looking at a comatose woman who was staring, unblinking, at the wall.

What do the dying see that so transfixes them? A minister friend calls it "Seeing the Light," and maybe she is right. Maybe I would call it "Seeing Life." Seeing Life even in a bare nursing home wall and being mesmerized by the fact that Life is gazing at itself. Fascinating. How could I have failed to notice this play of Life, this ever-moving unfolding of Life—even in a silent room at the nursing home where the clock ticks away precious seconds of life. The body is dying, yet Life lives. Amazing.

How could I have failed to notice the timelessness of Life?

## Wind on the Lake

If I were calm and lucid on my deathbed, what would be the niggling regrets or worries that might blow across the calm, spacious lake I see before me?

Would I worry about Bill? On the one hand, I know he can take care of himself. On the other hand, his choices of partners or of what he "should do" are too often based on other people's desires. As a younger brother, he acquiesces to people he wants to like him. May you be well, dear Bill. May you make good choices for yourself.

Would I worry about my grandchildren and their futures? Their parents have given them a good foundation. Chloe and Max, may you fare well.

What good friends would I want to see? Friends from long ago, friends whom, until now, I had forgotten how dear they are to me. My high school friends—Judi and Carolyn and other friends I have not kept up with.

How about my cousin Sharon? Five years older than me, she has always seemed like my big sister. I would love to see her now. I miss the heart connection to the teenager who taught eight-year-old me how to dance in her bedroom.

My dear open-hearted girlfriend, Mary Beth who lives in Portland, Oregon. She is like a sister. "Stay with me!" she e-mails every time I tell her I'm coming to Portland. This past March she planned my three precious days with her. While she went to work Friday morning, she sent her significant other, Les, out to breakfast with me at Bob's Red Mill—home of all those gluten-free flours and organic grains you never heard of. Saturday she and I went to see "Wicked," and Sunday we went to Carson Hot Springs, a 1920s-style spa.

After soaking in an old-fashioned claw-foot bathtub full of hot mineral water, the attendant leads you to a cot where she wraps you in cotton blankets for 25 more minutes of sweating so that you emerge with that deep-clean, detoxified feeling. That's the feeling I'd like to have on my deathbed. A detoxed life with detoxed memories, resting in the peace of nowhere to go and nothing to do. A feeling of unfinished business finally finished, loose ends let go.

What is the unfinished business? Unfinished business simply means deep feelings felt, tough feelings acknowledged and tenderized by acceptance. Letting go of what could have / would have / should have been. Letting go of regret and resentment. Letting go of a tightened, contracted, protected heart. Some people call this forgiveness.

I visited my father for one weekend every three months in the five years before he died. I didn't particularly like watching *Jeopardy* at seven on Friday nights, but I was stalking the daddy I had known once upon a time. Occasionally, this man of few words would say one sentence that rang deeply, and this turned out to be enough. When he said, "I wish I'd spent more time with you when you were kids," that was as close to asking forgiveness as he could get. And I forgave him. Spending his last six days with him and my siblings, I floated in a state of grace where any unfinished business was mysteriously finished.

My alcoholic mother? For years, I did everything I could to save her life—intervention, trips, books. I was there for her last eleven days, pleading for her guardian angel to take care of her. She was afraid to face Jesus after she had wasted half her life with the spirits in a bottle, so I begged her guardian angel to intercede for her spirit. I never cry when I visit my mother's grave. I have no regrets. I could not have done anything more.

What else would hold me back? Wishing I had done more meditation? That I had loved more? Been more present? Regrets are useless. There is only Now. Life unfolding. Energy moving in space. That's all it has ever been.

# Plop!

I TOOK THE TRAINING TO become a hospice volunteer when I was 45. My grandparents had died some years before, and my parents were healthy. *But really*, I thought, *how much longer can this go on? How long before death takes someone else I love?*

I wanted to prepare myself for death, and when, five years later, my father was dying, I was there at his home, giving personal care, which I could never have dreamed of doing otherwise. Spending my father's final week with him was one of the best things I have done in my life. Even though I was AWOL from work, still wrangling with my employer to get family leave approved, nevertheless I wasn't leaving my father's bedside, no matter how long it took. There, in the midst of my father's bedroom, his recliner in the living room, and the kitchen where I caught him eating pumpkin pie at four in the morning, my mind was completely content; there was nowhere else on earth I wanted to be.

As a Buddhist (although I didn't yet call myself that), I wanted to use the opportunity of my father's death to practice a "charnel ground" meditation, or as close as I could get to it in this society. I interviewed him for three mornings so that I could write his obituary. I stayed as close to his body as possible by doing his dialysis "exchanges" four times a day. The final morning I was in his bedroom at 5:00

a.m. draining liquid out of his abdomen. Then while the replacement liter of sterile solution was draining into his abdomen, I yoked my breath to his. Every time he breathed in, I breathed in. Every time he breathed out, I breathed out and sighed, "Ahh" as if he had lived a long, satisfactory life. He opened his eyes and looked at me in the dark, as if to say, *What are you doing, Sis?*—then closed his eyes and drifted off.

When the exchange was complete, I went back to bed, meditated for a few minutes, then began to doze. An hour later, my sister woke me up. Our father was dead.

I think of funeral homes as putting the bereaved family on the conveyor belt of how-everyone-does-a-funeral. Having talked with many hospice-trained friends, my possibilities widened considerably. All I had to do was ask. I had the confidence to push the envelope and keep my father's body at home for eight hours after death. I asked if I could dress the body, and surprisingly, my evangelical brother showed up to help me. That's when the two of us realized that the physical form on the gurney was not our father; it just looked like him. The next day, we were dry-eyed as we gave our eulogies.

When the funeral director showed my brother and me into the warehouse room where we were to dress our father's body, my brother asked, "Do you get many people who want to dress the dead body?" Because my father lived (and died) in the Corn Belt, we could nearly see the funeral director dancing around to answer this question and not hurt our feelings. "Well, there are Moslems and Hindus who come in and dress the body." That meant fewer than a handful of requests each year.

At the graveside, I stayed while everyone else went on to the luncheon at the church I grew up in. I watched the gravediggers take away the fake green-grass carpet, lower the casket, and back a dump truck-load of dirt up to the grave. Plop! My father, who had owned a construction company, was six feet under a big pile of dirt.

# I, Too

THE BUDDHA RECOMMENDS FIVE subjects for frequent reflection, and I have seriously taken up the Five Daily Recollections as contemplations at the end of my daily meditation. Over time, the recollections slowly, subtly take on a life of their own. When I go to visit a hospice client, I gaze at her wrinkled face and think, "I too am of the nature to grow old." This thought leads me directly to compassion, because I am not different than she is. In her, I am seeing a preview of my own coming attractions.

\* \* \*

### The Five Daily Recollections

I am of the nature to grow old. Aging is inevitable.
I am of the nature to become ill. Sickness is
   unavoidable.
I am of the nature to die. Death is unavoidable.
Everything I cherish will change and vanish.
Karma is the only thing I own.

\* \* \*

Because I travel frequently and go on meditation retreats for about eight weeks every year, I ask hospice to assign me short-term clients. I have visited several lonely old ladies in the nursing home.

One woman kept her eyes closed during my visit, perhaps because she didn't want to be bothered by a stranger. I simply sat beside her bed in the nursing home and thought, "I too am of the nature to become ill and feel poorly and not want to be bothered."

Visiting a friend's mother in the hospice room of the local nursing home, I could see that she was close to the end and that my friend, an only child, looked the worse for wear. Though she knew her mother's death was coming, she still had the hope, the mini-denial, that I have had myself: *Not yet. Later.* I looked at the mother, with her eyes closed, and thought, *I too am of the nature to die. Death is unavoidable.*

There was another eyes-closed nursing-home hospice client, a woman I visited only three times. I had been told she just needed someone to hold her hand. I moved a chair close to the bed, and soon found myself drawn halfway into bed with her, only my toes remaining on the floor. She had one bottle of body lotion sitting on her bedside table. *Everything I cherish will change and vanish*, I thought, *until I have only a bottle of lotion left.*

Over time, I found the Recollections migrating into my daily life. Driving into town one day, I poked along behind a really slow car. I couldn't even see the driver's head. *I too am of the nature to grow old*, I thought, *and drive really slowly.* That thought made me take my foot off the accelerator.

One time hospice called me on a Tuesday morning; I went to a house trailer on Tuesday afternoon where a number of adult children were arriving and expecting the professional (me) to take care of things. I was the most direct I have ever been: "Go sit in the bedroom with your mother. Say whatever you need to say." The mother died the next morning.

* * *

### The One-Day Hospice Client

Yesterday
angels hovered 'round
a woman in a trailer
crammed with sons, daughters,
grandchildren, and hope.

Today
white petals fall
from the family tree.
Bare branches
fragrant with flowers
buffeted by the winds
of departing wings.

# Peg:
# The Six-Year Hospice Patient

Because I used to be a psychotherapist, hospice sometimes assigns me patients who can use a little informal counseling, or people with complicated grief. (I am a bereavement volunteer as well as a patient volunteer.) In October, 2005, the hospice volunteer coordinator asked me to visit Peg because "she needs someone to talk to."

How would you feel if you walked into a home and met a woman your age who looked older than your mother? I was shocked. I was polite. I was repulsed. I directed my mind toward compassion. After all, that's the reason I volunteer for hospice. It was much easier to feel gratitude for my own good health.

Peg had been a drinker and a smoker. Now she had chronic obstructive pulmonary disease (COPD) and an additional respiratory infection. The COPD caused her severe anxiety about her breathing. The idea that I might have to do something with the oxygen machine while Peg's husband was out of the house caused me some anxiety, even though I had a sheet of instructions.

Sam had taken care of his dying mother, his dying father, his dying uncle, and now his dying wife. He had the patience of Job. Recently retired from the post office job he had had for 35 years, Sam would not leave Peg alone.

Perhaps it would be more accurate to say that Peg did not want to be left alone; she would become quite anxious about "what if" something happened while Sam was out.

Peg's first hospice volunteer began visiting four months before I did. Helen was almost old enough to be Peg's mother. Having six children of her own and a clan of grandchildren and greats, Helen is a community-minded, openhearted woman who has endured the loss of several children and grandchildren. Peg had six cats, so Helen often brought Peg stuffed animals or other little gifts she knew would tickle Peg. Helen sat with Peg on Wednesday evenings in the fall, winter, and spring while Sam went bowling, the only social event in Sam's life.

When I arrived at Peg and Sam's cabin on Tuesday afternoons at two, the television was always on. Peg sat in her wheelchair watching TV while the oxygen machine wheezed nearby. After some weeks of talking to Peg with the TV on, I asked whether it could be muted. Even so, my eyes still drifted to the TV and glued themselves there no matter how mindfully I tried to keep my attention on Peg. Eventually I asked Peg if she could turn off the TV when I arrived, and Sam showed me which remote to use and which buttons to push. From then on, Sam always turned off the TV the minute I walked into the living room. He then departed to run errands—picking up a prescription or going grocery shopping. Because Peg had a history of prescription-drug abuse, Sam had to pick up her prescription of morphine weekly. Otherwise, Peg would overuse it and there wouldn't be any left for the last few days of the month, before she could get a refill.

Peg told me that her bladder had collapsed, so the doctor had created a mesh hammock in her vagina in which to suspend the bladder, and then sewed up her vagina. Peg felt terrible about not being able to have a sexual relationship with her husband, Sam. I wondered how he felt about kissing a woman with only seven snaggly black teeth, a woman who looked twenty years older than him.

During our first few months, Peg confided that she and her older sister, Mary, had been sexually molested by their stepfather, Gary. Mary was now an alcoholic who seldom came to visit Peg because she couldn't bear to see her younger sister in this condition. Both Mary's children were also alcoholics.

Peg's mother had died a few years before, but her 80-year-old stepfather, Gary, occasionally stopped by with his 78-year-old girlfriend, Virginia, to visit. Peg loved Virginia, but was never that keen on seeing Gary. Peg also told me that her younger brother, the son of Gary and her mother, had killed himself twenty years earlier.

Peg had had two abusive marriages and a child with each husband before she met Sam. They had been together for thirty years. One thing I admired about Peg: her two adult children had both been to vocational schools and were happily married and solidly middle class, despite Peg's own lower-socioeconomic-class upbringing.

During the first several months, I sometimes asked pointed questions: "What would you do if this were your last anniversary with Sam?" "How would you celebrate Thanksgiving if this were your last Thanksgiving?" "Have you talked with Sam about where you want to be buried?"

In the spring, hospice assigned another volunteer to visit Peg in order to give Sam more respite. Trudy visited Peg on Thursday afternoons. She would hold Peg's hand for two hours while Peg fell asleep on the sofa with the TV on. In our quarterly team meetings, Trudy seemed unhappy with this arrangement, but unable to change the situation. On the other hand, Trudy picked up cues that I was oblivious to. "I'm sure Peg is sneaking cigarettes," she said.

"With an oxygen tank in the room?" I asked with raised eyebrows.

"I'm sure of it. Don't you smell the smoke?" Trudy replied.

I didn't, but I believed Trudy. Peg did chug her water bottle as if it were a long-neck bottle of beer.

Occasionally, a hospice nurse would be assigned to Peg for a month or two, but then they would sign her off. Eventually the town nurse made weekly visits. A visiting physical therapist assigned Peg the exercise of walking from the sofa to the kitchen, but I never saw her attempt it. We talked for two years about going to the dentist before Peg made an appointment. When she finally received her false teeth, I saw her wear them once.

After six months of weekly visits, I tiptoed into the Five Daily Recollections by leading Peg through the first reflection, unsure of what her response would be. "I am of the nature to grow old. Aging is unavoidable."

\* \* \*

# I Am of the Nature to Grow Old

My hair is of the nature to grow old.
My brain is of the nature to grow old.
My eyes are of the nature to grow old.
My ears are of the nature to grow old.
My teeth and gums are of the nature to grow old.
My double chin is of the nature to grow old
   and sag.
My neck is of the nature to grow old.

My shoulders are of the nature to grow old.
My upper arms are of the nature to grow old
   and sag.
My elbows are of the nature to grow old.
My wrists are of the nature to grow old.
My hands are of the nature to grow old.
My fingers are of the nature to grow old.

My heart and circulatory system are of the nature
   to grow old.
My lungs are of the nature to grow old.
My breasts are of the nature to grow old and sag.
My digestive system is of the nature to grow old.
My elimination system is of the nature to
   grow old.
My bladder is of the nature to grow old and leak.
My uterus is of the nature to grow old.
My vagina is of the nature to grow old.
My belly is of the nature to grow old.

My hips and pelvis are of the nature to grow old.
My back is of the nature to grow old.
My bones are of the nature to grow old.

My legs are of the nature to grow old.
My knees are of the nature to grow old.
My joints are of the nature to grow old.
My ankles are of the nature to grow old.
My feet are of the nature to grow old.
My toes and toenails are of the nature to grow old.
My skin is of the nature to grow old.
My appearance is of the nature to grow old.
I am of the nature to grow old. Aging is inevitable.
I am of the nature to be the oldest person in the room.
I am of the nature to have knees that sound like loose ball bearings.
I am of the nature to have to sit down while I am putting on my shoes.
I am of the nature to walk bent over.
I am of the nature to be unable to remember names of people or places.

\* \* \*

To tell the truth, I needed the contemplation on aging myself in order to simply look at Peg and her seven remaining snaggleteeth. Her naturally wavy gray hair could be very becoming, but often she could not lean over the sink for Sam to wash it without having an anxiety attack about her breathing. She could not stand up by herself. She whined. She asked Sam to heat up her tea, to refresh her water bottle, to bring her a tissue. She was completely homebound and sofa-bound except for going to doctors' appointments every few months.

Peg knew that I taught meditation classes, so she thought that I was trying out these contemplations on her that I also taught to my class. She had taken many classes at the community college, but never earned an associate's degree. This belief that she was helping me seemed to give her a sense of purpose—and here I had thought I was helping *her*.

After a month of doing the aging contemplation on every visit, I added the next reflection: "I am of the nature to become sick. Illness is unavoidable."

\* \* \*

# I Am of the Nature to Become Ill

I am of the nature to become ill. Sickness is
 unavoidable.
I am of the nature to have disease.
I am of the nature to have dis-ease.
I am of the nature to feel weak.
I am of the nature to feel queasy.
I am of the nature to feel achy.
I am of the nature to feel tired.
I am of the nature to feel pain.
I am of the nature to feel listless.
I am of the nature to feel sorry for myself.
I am of the nature to feel depressed.
I am of the nature to feel unpleasant.
I am of the nature to be irritable.
I am of the nature to have a headache.
I am of the nature to have a stomachache.
I am of the nature to feel out of sorts.
I am of the nature to have night sweats.
I am of the nature to feel torpor.
I am of the nature to feel malaise.
I am of the nature to have a fever.
I am of the nature to feel nauseous.
I am of the nature to feel dizzy.
I am of the nature to lose my appetite.
I am of the nature to be constipated.
I am of the nature to be irregular.

* * *

I am of the nature to become ill.[2]
I am of the nature to have dis-ease.
I am of the nature to become blemished.
I am of the nature to become sun-damaged.
I am of the nature to have viruses.
I am of the nature to have "bugs."
I am of the nature to wilt.
I am of the nature to have brown spots.
I am of the nature to wither.
I am of the nature to become blighted.
I am of the nature to have dis-ease.
Dis-ease is unavoidable.
Sickness is unavoidable.
Illness is unavoidable.
I am of the nature to have dis-ease.

\* \* \*

---

2 *The Meditative Gardener: Cultivating Mindfulness of Body, Feelings, and Mind* (Putney, VT: Heart Path Press, 2010), 160.

After a month of doing the aging and the illness reflection together with Peg, I added the contemplation on death. "I am of the nature to die. Death is unavoidable." I personalized this contemplation to fit Peg's situation. Her many cats had disappeared one by one until only two remained.

"Just like my cats, I am of the nature to die.

"Just like my grandparents, I am of the nature to die.

"Just like my aunts and uncles, I am of the nature to die.

"Just like my mother, I too am of the nature to die.

"Like my brother, I too am of the nature to die."

Over her sofa hung a picture of Jesus knocking on a door. So I closed this contemplation, "Just like Jesus, I too am of the nature to die."

The next month, I added the contemplation "Everything I cherish will change and vanish." Like her cats, Peg's gardens had all but disappeared. Yellowing leaves on the trees outside the picture window were falling to the ground.

After two and a half years, just before I left for my annual one-month retreat, Peg weighed 79 pounds and looked like she was ninety years old. She was now "seeing" her dead brother every day, and she was happy about these visitations. I assumed I would not see her again, yet when I returned home a month later, she was still alive.

Because of COPD, Peg had severe anxiety. She was extremely afraid to get into the car to go to a doctor's appointment because that involved a changeover from her main oxygen tank to her small, portable oxygen tank. She also worried that she would have the urge to urinate. Her re-suspended bladder seemed to put a crimp in urination, so she was never sure when she was "done." She might finish and get back into her wheelchair, only to feel that she needed the toilet or portable commode again.

Peg's primary-care doctor didn't seem very responsive to all the complications of Peg's situation, but Peg and Sam loyally continued to go to him as if they had no other options. When one of her infrequent doctor's appointments was on a Tuesday afternoon (the time of my regular visit), I talked her though the transition from wheelchair to car. "Notice sitting in your wheelchair . . . Notice that Sam is changing over your oxygen tanks . . . Notice that Sam is helping you stand up . . . Notice that you are sitting down on the car seat." Then while Sam ran around and packed the wheelchair into the trunk and got everything else in order, I sat on a sliver of car seat beside Peg, directing her to notice her body and her sensations. I directed her to notice how anxiety felt in her body, how worry felt. I drove my own car to her doctor's office and talked her through each movement out of the car and into the doctor's office.

During my third year with Peg, she was taken off one of her ten prescriptions, and she began to gain weight. After several months she weighed 120 pounds. At our team meeting, Trudy suggested less-frequent visits. "This woman is not dying." So the four of us volunteers began to visit every other week.

By this time, Peg settled on the body scan as her favorite meditation. After chatting for about half an hour, she would ask if I had time to do the body scan. I always did.

I sat in her wheelchair next to the faded blue sofa where she would be sitting. She lived on that sofa, day and night, so she would just lift her legs up, and lean back on a small mountain of pillows so that she was in a slightly reclining position, with a C-shaped neck pillow supporting her neck and another pillow under her head. She would tuck her newest stuffed animal into the crook of her arm, and then close her eyes.

"Notice the body relaxing," I would say. "Bring your attention to your head, resting on a pillow . . . your neck . . . your back resting on the sofa." She would reach out to hold my hand, but instead of holding hands in midair for twenty minutes, I would gently place her hand by her side, and as I continued giving instructions, I slowly, slowly withdrew my hand. "Notice your legs, perhaps feeling the slight pressure of your pants legs resting on your skin. Notice the pressure of the heels on the sofa. Now bring your attention to your toes. Notice any sensations in your toes."

Over the course of twenty minutes, I would slowly work my way up the legs, hips, torso, arms, and head. She usually fell into a fitful sleep with her legs twitching so dramatically, I thought she would fall off the sofa. If she woke up before I left, she felt quite relaxed and refreshed.

Guiding these body scans was really what made these visits interesting for me. Trudy, the volunteer who held Peg's hand for two hours while Peg slept with the TV on, burned out after four years because those sorts of visits were just too unsatisfactory for her. But the body scans nourished me and were obviously serving Peg by reducing her anxiety about breathing and reducing the pain of her fibromyalgia, so I was willing to go on and on, even though hospice reduced our volunteer visits to once a month. I made a CD of the body scan for Peg, but she never listened to it.

After more than six years of visiting Peg, the end came surprisingly quickly. One night in December 2011, Emergency Medical Services (EMS) came and took Peg to the hospital, and, as usual, Peg returned home three or four days later. The discharge plans called for a hospice nurse; she visited once, but saw no need to come again. The night after my January visit, EMS came and took Peg to the emergency room. Two days later, I received a call that Peg was in the hospital and would not be going home.

I arrived at the ICU room that Friday afternoon to find Peg lying open-mouthed and comatose on the bed. Sitting in the room with her were her husband, Sam; her son and his wife; her daughter and her daughter's half sister; Peg's sister, Mary; and her step-father, Gary, and his girlfriend, Virginia; as well as the minister who had administered Reiki to Peg every Friday for the past seven years, and three of us hospice volunteers. All these people were chatting with each other, so I went to stand on the uncrowded side of the bed and began to whisper a twenty-minute body scan into Peg's ear. Her monitor began to beep, and the minister said, "Cheryl, you are definitely having an effect on her." Peg's vital signs were slowing down, so Sam asked for the monitor to be turned off. He didn't need to see her numbers going down. The hospice choir, Hallowell, arrived and sang several songs before I left the completely packed room for my Friday evening engagements.

The next morning was snowy and slow driving, so I didn't get to the hospital until 9:30 a.m. Sam, Peg's daughter, and the daughter's half-sister were relaxing in the family waiting room, so I sat alone with Peg in her room and put my hand on her cool hand. Once again I led her through her body scan, although I did not really expect that she could feel her body anymore. "Perhaps your body feels the same as the bed," I said. "Perhaps the body is just a bunch of twinkling lights in space. Why, look at that!"

As I went through the twenty-minute body scan, I could hear a monitor beeping at the nursing station outside Peg's room. I kissed her goodbye, and bid farewell to Sam and to Peg's daughter.

Peg died forty minutes later.

www.ingramcontent.com/pod-product-compliance
Lightning Source LLC
Chambersburg PA
CBHW032337300426
44109CB00041B/1137